NEW ZEALAND'S
NATIONAL PARKS

NEW ZEALAND'S NATIONAL PARKS

LEONARD COBB JAMES DUNCAN

(bfp) Books For Pleasure

A division of Paul Hamlyn Limited
Sydney, Auckland, London, New York.

Acknowledgements:
The authors acknowledge with appreciation the assistance we have received in the course of producing this book from: Tom Pitman, David Lowe, David De Gray, David Wakelin, Bruce Postill, John Ward (Mt Cook Airlines), Ian Blackmore, Jack Drydon, John Mazey, Geof Moon, Ray Cleland.

We express particular thanks and affection to Inge Cobb and Pat Duncan for simply standing by during difficulties, for their encouragement and for their practical help. We also thank John, Norman and Martina Cobb and Andrew and Linda Duncan for their tolerance.

This book is dedicated to the ideal of National Parks as a compact between man and nature and to universal understanding that it is man who must ensure the survival of the compact.

End Papers:

The Maori legend of the creation is depicted in this illustration. In the beginning was nothing and then were created Rangi the sky and Papa the earth. They lay in close embrace as man and wife and gave birth to many children. Tane, the god of the forest, made space to walk upon the earth by separating Rangi and Papa in a great test of strength. Today the sorrow of their parting is still seen in mist and rain.

Front Illustration: Eternal snow and luxuriant rain forest present the unforgettable contrast of Westland National Park.

Title Page: The road to Milford Sound. At every curve there is another magnificent sight.

Opposite: New Zealand lichens and mosses are among the most abundant in nature, having developed in rain forest ranging from sub-tropical to sub-antarctic in type. Conditions in these forests have encouraged proliferation of plants like the umbrella mosses, *Mniodendron*, which thrive on moist forest floors or rotting logs.

Published by Paul Hamlyn Ltd.
31 Airedale Street.
Auckland, New Zealand.
First Published 1980
© Copyright. James Duncan. Leonard Cobb.
Typeset in New Zealand by Auckland Typographic Services.
ISBN 0 7296 0214 1
Printed in Hong Kong.
Designer: Leonard Cobb.

T. Pitman

Contents

The Dobson Nature Walk introduces Arthur's Pass National Park visitors to a wealth of alpine plants.

Introduction

Over an unimaginable span of time, the islands of New Zealand developed a specialised, often unique, variety of life, with plants and birds which had no counterpart elsewhere. Only here did a reptile from the age of dinosaurs survive. There were no animal predators because they arose after New Zealand had separated from other land masses. Browsing animals were also absent, so that the New Zealand forest was able to become a dense blanket protecting a steep land from erosion.

New Zealand had 65 million years of solitude in which to evolve its great beauty and its distinctive forms of life. Man has destroyed much of it in less than 200 years.

The establishment of New Zealand's National Parks stands out in brilliant contrast to this recent history. They preserve a significant part of the beauty which made New Zealand one of the most fortunately endowed countries on earth.

There is nothing more precious than National Parks among New Zealand's resources. Yet they are fragile, for they exist only on the strength of an idea – the idea that we need wilderness for itself, for ourselves and for people who come after us. As long as that idea stays alive in people's minds, the parks are safe from interference. This book is written to help keep that idea alive.

The recoil of nature from man began in New Zealand long ago with the extinction of the giant moa and the introduction of the kiore, a rat found throughout Polynesia, which had some effect on birdlife. The Great Migration of the Maori brought more pressure on forest and bird but the Maori were careful to stay within well-defined bounds, for they needed the forest. Their effects were minimal but the second great migration of settlers from Europe to New Zealand radically changed the landscape, with the wholesale destruction of forest which had stood for thousands of years and nurtured specialised birds like the kiwi, weka, kokako, kakapo, takahe and huia, some of which became extinct. Severe erosion of steep hillsides followed on a large scale.

But the introduction of new ways to New Zealand was late enough to permit some profit from the mistakes of others. The national park concept of protecting the wilderness was born in the United States of America in the 1870's and New Zealand was one of the first countries to emulate the example. The Maori, who traditionally held land in common ownership, created the first New Zealand National Park. At that time, the appreciation which we have today of protecting the close and interdependent relationship between living things was not marked, but at least the idea of keeping development away from areas of fine scenery had been realised.

The National Parks system grew only slowly but in view of the dim appreciation of what man was doing to the New Zealand environment otherwise, it was surprising that it grew at all. The difficulty of turning some of New Zealand's wilderness into farms undoubtedly helped. As the system grew, so did the crassness with which economic development was pursued. It was natural for the early settlers to regard New Zealand's forests as an enemy to be destroyed because they needed desperately to make a living for themselves in a new land. But their attitude implanted in New Zealanders a deep regard for progress with little regard for natural beauty.

We should remind ourselves regularly of what we did in the past for those who do not know their history are condemned to re-live it. We have burned bush and killed birds which depended on it for survival, we have slowed and dirtied streams and rivers, we have interfered with lakes, we have extinguished geysers, we have drowned thermal areas. National Parks have, unfortunately, not been excluded from these depredations. Look around – Lake Monowai raised, Lake Waikaremoana lowered, Lake Pukaki raised, Lake Tekapo raised, Lake Hawea raised, Aratiatia Rapids tamed, Wairakei's Geyer Valley destroyed, the Devil's Eyeglass bulldozed, Orakei Korako drowned, Tongariro and Arthur's Pass National Parks compromised by electricity transmission pylons. New Zealand has much beauty still, as this book shows, and we boast of it to overseas visitors, yet there is much sadness too when we contemplate what has been lost.

A good deal of the damage has been done during the search for electricity generation. It has been led by successive governments on whose ultimate trusteeship we depend for the protection of natural resources. The Lake Manapouri episode shows how unreliable that trusteeship can be and how vulnerable to development are even the most beautiful and unspoiled areas of New Zealand. Only sustained and vigorous public protest stopped successive governments from raising the lake level for power production, a rise being fundamental to a government invitation to establish the project. A power station went ahead but a few protest leaders rallied massive support to prevent Lake Manapouri from suffering the ugly fate of Lake Monowai, with its foreshore ruined by the stumps of trees which will take hundred of years to decay and disappear.

The danger of such interference will persist as long as governments put economic aims ahead of beauty and the present emphasis on economic growth and new energy-intensive industries spells great danger for our National Parks. The Manapouri issue also raised serious questions about the independent role of the National Parks Authority and the protective powers of individual park boards. The Nature Conservation Council also proved to be ineffective in its opposition to raising the lake. The weight of government influence on these bodies has an inhibiting effect on their independence. Yet there is no doubt that New Zealand needs strong nature conservancy organisations if we are not to lose, little by little, the unspoiled country we have left.

The tragedy of New Zealand today is the widespread replacement of our beautiful, luxuriant, unique native forest with sterile, exotic pine forests. The pace at which this is proceeding, encouraged by the State and by a Forest Service which seems to have little regard for its rightful role as a conservator of forests, is perturbing and suggests that eventually only our National Parks will, if left alone, harbour the forest of Tane which so much makes the New Zealand landscape what it is. That would produce a great imbalance in the landscape.

Encroachment on National Parks may be gradual but in the end it can only destroy or adulterate the wilderness. The great volcanic wonder of Mt Ruapehu illustrates the problems facing park boards in encouraging us to use and understand the parks without allowing the debasement of what makes us want to visit them in the first place. Haphazard siting of ski club huts on the mountainside has badly scarred a former wilderness area and damaged the local environment. More recently, there have been problems on the other side of the mountain with the development of the Turoa skifield.

A great difficulty lies in reaching agreement on what is a mutually-acceptable middle course between park boards and developers. There may be no acceptable middle course. Perhaps the only safeguard is to restrict all but minimal development like tracks, huts and day shelters to outside the park boundries.

The introduction of browsing animals to New Zealand's forests and alpine grasslands has proved to be one the major environmental disasters of the last 200 years. New Zealand forest evolved over a very long time in the absence of browsing animals and it has been shown to be absolutely defenceless against them. Wild goats, deer and opossums have been the main culprits, stripping away undergrowth which acts as a nursery for new trees and which prevents erosion on the steep hill country of New Zealand. The use of helicopters to hunt deer has been the greatest single contribution to the regeneration of forests and one can only hope that extermination remains a foreseeable objective, with all other deer safely penned up in farms. And only research and determination will exterminate the opossum as we exterminated the wild rabbit. If as much attention had been paid to the aesthetic, recreational and conservation value of native forest as to the economic value of introduced grass, we would have ensured the preservation of National Park bush in its original state.

The hunters who insist that we must retain a stable wild deer population for recreational purposes may have sharp eyes over a rifle sight but they are missing the seriousness of the impact which deer have on native forest. Deer and healthy native bush are incompatible and the National Parks should not be used as game reserves.

National Parks are, in the words of the National Parks Act, there to 'preserve in perpetuity for the benefit and enjoyment of the public, areas of New Zealand that contain scenery of such distinctive quality or natural features so beautiful or unique that their preservation is in the national interest.' There are some purely physical matters which fit this prescription, such as the protection of forests and birds and streams and lakes. There are scientific aspects to this protection too. They are fairly self-evident because they can be examined in the parks themselves.

There is also something just as important but less easily-defined – the value of wilderness areas to our spirit. Anyone who has heard older people speaking with real sadness about the passing of the huia will know just how valuable can be our sense of identity with the natural world about us. National Parks give us the best opportunities to develop such a sense of identity. And they show us natural communities which are not haphazard collections of plants, birds, insects and marine life but carefully-balanced systems which have been arrived at after aeons of experimentation and slow adjustment. They are highly developed and we must treat them so.

National Parks offer vast contrasts to our cities, towns, managed rural lands and exotic forests. Their beauty and grandeur cannot be duplicated or replaced. They offer us horizons which can reinstate the scale of the world before we reduced it with car and jet aircraft. Take away the car and the road, leave the track and the path and suddenly before you is the kind of challenge to your courage, endurance and spirit which faced the first explorers. You may with luck travel two or three kilometres a day in the heaviest bush of Fiordland and in doing so you will be replacing your usual horizons with something far more exciting. We need the opportunity to walk over a ridge which leads to another ridge and another

after that, without the feeling that we are about to emerge into cleared farmland or town or highway. That is the essence of the recreational value of National Parks.

Although New Zealand is a small country, it is famous for its variety, for being a place where there is always something a little different around the corner. It's true and National Parks reveal the differences. You can descend from the ice and snow of the Southern Alps in Westland National Park and slip into a hot natural pool in the Copland Valley to dissolve away tiredness. You can crunch ice underfoot on a glacier, walk through a wild landscape where the earth oozes out in steam and mud, swim in the world's clearest water, take the longest ski-run around or stay for days or weeks within rain forest.

This book is not intended as other than a general introduction to New Zealand's National Parks, for such diversity cannot be contained in a single book. The plants, birds and geology of National Parks are dealt with in detail in park handbooks which are essential to the proper enjoyment of each park. Other publications have specialised information on plants and birds. The visitor centres at each National Park should be a compulsory first stop if you are to appreciate the most essential features of the parks and there you can obtain a range of pamphlets with detailed information.

Words and photographs can do no more than show you a glimpse or two of our National Parks. Treat them as the start of a journey. And take with you someone young for the young will have to learn lessons others have already learned if our National Parks are to remain wilderness areas which are within man's reach but beyond his grasp.

Tongariro National Park

It is a choice historical irony that a Maori chief should have given New Zealanders their first national park. In one magnificent gesture, he took the land away from the stretching hands of the pakeha and then returned it, in a sense which was well ahead of its time.

It is also an irony that the gift was partly a response to the covetous motives of others of his own race.

Yet let the name of Te Heuheu IV Horonuku be honoured for his gift of not only the great volcanoes of the central North Island, but also the concept that the land has a spiritual value above that of ownership. That is the concept behind all of our National Parks and Horonuku's gift gave it potency in the minds of New Zealanders.

Tongariro National Park is, by its physical prominence, a conspicuous reminder of early Maori identification with the land. To them these mountains were sacred, tapu, and a strong element in legend.

It is easy to imagine the awe, the profound impact which must have attended the first meeting between the Maori and these mountains. Even today, when main highways routinely carry people past the mountain flanks, they remain striking examples of the earth's violent strength.

Rising abruptly as they do from a relatively flat plain, they impose on your eyes a bulk which arouses wonder. Their volcanic nakedness gives them an impact of a unique kind.

Sacredness falls fittingly on these mountains.

The high priest of the Arawa canoe must have felt so when he journeyed south from the Bay of Plenty landing place and laid claim to them. Centuries passed before his descendants, the Tuwharetoa, arrived to take possession and fought a long and bitter war to defeat the Ngati Hotu then in residence.

Threatening the landscape it helped to build, Ngauruhoe vents ash, gas and rock from the deep fires of Ruaumoko, the earthquake god. Hot rock fragments cascade down the mountainside, a reminder that the violence which created the parkland is not far below the golden tussock.

Tongariro National Park

The final battle was fought near the small volcanic cone of Pukekaikiore on the western side of Ngauruhoe and visible from State Highway 47. Its name is a chilling reminder of the consequent celebration – 'the hill where the human rats were eaten'.

The origins of the park lie in a quarrel for possession of the mountains. In the 1880s, recriminations over the land wars of 1860-72 were still continuing. Horonuku had helped Waikato against the settlers and his assistance to the guerilla Te Kooti, after his arrival at Tokaanu in 1869, had further compromised Horonuku and his people. At the same time, the land-hunger of the European settlers was becoming evident in the district. They were eyeing the tussock lands for grazing.

In 1886 a sitting of the Maori Land Court at Taupo threatened the Tuwharetoa hold on the mountains. The Whanganui chief, Te Rangihiwinui Taitoko, widely known as Major Kemp, had fought on the side of the English Queen against his own race and he pressed a case for declaring Tuwharetoa land to be rebel land. He also claimed to have lit his cooking fires on the land.

With telling metaphor, Horonuku pointed from the courthouse to Tongariro, which just then threw out smoke, and exclaimed: 'There, see my fire!' He won his point but he could foresee further trouble ahead from the pakeha settlers. He called a special meeting of his tribe, which agreed to a proposal that the mountain tops be given to the Crown as a reserve for all the people of New Zealand.

On September 23rd, 1887, a deed of gift was drawn up at the Taupo Native Land Court. The original rough document was later replaced by a tidier version, a copy of which is displayed in the park headquarters. Te Heuheu signed as Te Heuheu Tukino, his given name, which he had changed to Horonuku (landslide) in respect for the memory of his father, who had been killed by a landslide.

It is interesting that Horonuku used the term national park when making the gift. Perhaps it was in emulation of the establishment of the world's first national park, Yellowstone, in the United States in 1872.

Even so, the gift was a remarkable example of foresight at a time when New Zealand development was being pioneered and the axe and the match were prime items in the national culture. In 1894, when Tongariro National Park was formally constituted by Act of Parliment, it was possible for a Minister of Lands, John McKenzie, to cite the uselessness of the land for grazing as a reason for turning it into a park.

The Act gave New Zealanders a park of 2630 ha. It did not include the topmost peak of Ruapehu. The adjacent, lower peak of Paretetaitonga was the southern point of Tuwharetoa ownership, the southwest and southeast of the mountain belonging to the Ngati Uenuku. The name of their former chief, Topia Turoa, is applied to the southern Ruapehu ski fields. Another oddity is that the name of Ngauruhoe did not appear on the original gift deed – it was included as part of Tongariro, to which the Tuwharetoa had always attached more importance. Geologically speaking, the Maori were correct, as Ngauruhoe has grown out of Tongariro.

The park was gradually extended and now covers 75,259 ha, the most recent addition being Pihanga, the volcanic peak just south of Turangi, and the nearby crater lake, Rotopounamu.

The continuing volcanic and thermal activity of the mountains gives the park a specific dramatic quality shared by no other. They stand aloof on their own ground, clear of visual competitors. Their mood can be sombre, fantastic, beautiful, strange, gathering power from a landscape visibly formed by an immense gushing of liquid rock from the earth over a period of some two million years.

There is no more arresting sight than these mountains glittering with snow while Ngauruhoe spins its eternal aerial wreath.

The volcanoes of the park occur at the southern extremity of a chain which stretches more than 1600 km across the Pacific Ocean. Their craters lie in a notably narrow band along a line which continues north from Ruapehu through Ngauruhoe, Tongariro, the Rotorua thermal and volcanic area, White Island and the volcanoes of the Kermadec Islands and Tonga. Pihanga and Tauhara, east of Taupo township, are also on this line.

Like a vision from the earth's dawn, the mountains seem to float above a plain of cloud. Seen from Pinnacle Ridge on Ruapehu, Ngauruhoe steams above the older shape of Tongariro behind it.

Sub-alpine grassland clings to an inhospitable country of volcanic rock which often becomes extremely hot in summer. All around, the shape of the land is as it has welled up from the interior of the earth. The ridges in the middle distance are great lava flows of Ruapehu, blanketed here and there by ever-questing plant life. Similar ridges sweep down from Tongariro (left) and Ngauruhoe.

A riven, blasted landscape pitted by craters: In the foreground, Blue Lake fills an old crater on Tongariro. The Emerald Lakes fill two more immediately below the cleft of the Red Crater, which is still active. To the right of Blue Lake is the steep side of the North Crater, with a flash of red rock a sign of the minerals which add colour to the lakes. Ngauruhoe puffs out its banner while Ruapehu's greater height is marked by the last of winter's snow.

Lyric Studios

The Maori made the connection, for one of the Tuwharetoa legends says that the Arawa canoe high priest, Ngatoroirangi, called for fire from Hawaiki when he was freezing on the mountain tops while examining the strange sight of snow and performing the sacred ceremonies required when taking possession of a new land. The fire gods of the North responded by sending fire which burst forth at White Island, Rotorua, Tarawera and Taupo before spouting from Tongariro.

This incident gave two of the park's mountains their names.

Ngatoroirangi called out to his ancestral spirits and sisters, who enlisted the aid of the gods, that he was being seized or carried away (riro) by the cold wind from the south (tonga).

A slave named Ngauruhoe who was fortunate enough to witness this miraculous event paid an unfortunate price - she was thrown as an offering to the fire gods into the erupting crater of the peak which bears her name.

Within and around the park is sufficient raw material for all the myth-making of which the Maori was capable. One legend explains the disappearance from the area of its second highest mountain.

Long ago, Pihanga, the beautiful maiden (this is quite apparent from her shape) was wooed by four warrior mountains. They decided to fight for her hand and their passion melted the rock in their bowels and they sent forth smoke and steam as they prepared for the battle. They fought with fire and molten rock, and Tongariro won Pihanga as his wife. The other mountains, unable to bear the huge mana of Tongariro, departed. In the night, Putauaki fled 160 km to the northern end of Kaiangaroa Plain. He is now called Edgecumbe. Tauhara dawdled his way sadly and painfully and by dawn had got only as far as the northern shore of Lake Taupo. Taranaki travelled in fury to the western edge of the land where he was named Egmont by Captain Cook.

On his way Taranaki gouged out the path of the Wanganui River and early Europeans in the district claimed that some Maori would not live on the line between Ruapehu and Taranaki in case the latter might seek a rematch.

Ruapehu (2796 m) is the highest mountain in the North Island, has the most northerly glaciers in New Zealand and looms largest in the park. Viewed from the Desert Road, it clearly demonstrates the flow of molten rock which formed it.

The mountain has an uncertain temper and an apt name (rua: hole; pehu: to explode). It is by no means dying down in activity and in 1954 it erupted violently, blasting out the summit crater to a depth of 350 m and expelling steam and huge, dark clouds of ash which fell as far off as Wellington, 240 km away.

The lake in the crater is a cloudy green, kept

warm by volcanic steam and it sometimes shows sulphur scum on the surface. It is easily accessible – only a three-hour climb from the top of State Highway 48 (New Zealand's highest) but beware. It can boil and throw mud over the surrounding ice and snow. It has caused one of New Zealand's worst disasters.

The lake overflows through a tunnel in the ice to create the sulphurous Wangaehu River, which passes under the main North Island trunk railway at Tangiwai. On Christmas Eve, 1953, a barrier of volcanic ash near the tunnel entrance gave way and the lake water burst out and down the Wangaehu, carrying with it huge boulders. The mass arrived at the Tangiwai rail bridge shortly before the night express from Wellington to Auckland and smashed the massive concrete piers. The train plunged through the bridge into the river and 151 people died.

The name Tangiwai means weeping waters and derives from the river's reputation for sudden floods.

Similar flows of volcanic mud and rocks, called lahars, have deposited small, conical hills alongside State Highway 48 near the start of its climb through the park. Walk around these (display boards explain their nature), look up the ring plain slope at Ruapehu and imagine the momentum which carried the material so far down the mountain. It is an impressive thought.

An angry burst from unpredictable Ruapehu has stained with mud the snow around the crater and sent a flow of mud and water down the mountainside. Such flows on a larger scale have created the lahars, mounds of avalanche material, which surround the mountains. Beyond Ruapehu is Hauhangatahi (1518 m), another of the park's volcanic cones.

Thousands of years of volcanic activity are shown in this photograph of Ruapehu from near the junction of State Highways 47 and 48. The small hills on the tussock plain are lahar mounds, formed from avalanches of snow, water, mud and rock down the mountainsides. Those in the foreground are part of a nature walk by SH 48, which climbs up the mountain. Larger lahars can be seen above the bush, along with the shapes of old lava flows.

Tongariro National Park

Tongariro National Park

A diversity of volcanic and thermal activity on the three big mountains provides a view of some of the forces which shaped our planet. The two Tama Lakes on the saddle between Ruapehu and Ngauruhoe are enormous explosion craters and the walk to them from the park headquarters takes you across the bare rock (very hot in summer) they threw out.

Tongariro (1948 m) is, like Ruapehu, an old volcano and has a complex structure, built up from many outlets. The most visible sign of the earlier nature of this quiescent giant, with its truncated cone hinting at some monstrous eruption long ago, is the Ketetahi Springs on the northern side. Here are steam vents, hot springs, many-coloured rocks and a primeval atmosphere which can become forbidding when mist or cloud is hanging on the wall of the north crater which sails above. The Maori valued the springs for their therapeutic qualities. The climb is steep but there are views over Lake Roto-a-Ira, Pihanga and the surrounding country to compensate you.

The thermal area of Ketetahi Springs makes a gash on the northern side of Tongariro. Continuously active, the springs spill and eject steam and scalding water which colours the rocks with fantastic hues.

Tongariro National Park

The craters of Tongariro show many different aspects of the nature of volcanoes. A sulphur lagoon, soda springs, the active Te Mari Crater, the vivid Blue Lake, the Emerald Lakes and the Red Crater set in an unworldly landscape provide a series of attractions for trampers and walkers.

Ngauruhoe (2290 m) is the kind of symmetrical cone we usually associate with volcanoes. It is the most continuously active volcano in New Zealand. Its clear shape and eternal wisp of steam, make it one of the most stirring sights of the south Pacific, by summer or winter. Every few years since records began it has erupted steam and ash and, in 1949 and 1954, lava flows, the latter being the biggest lava eruption recorded in New Zealand. The lava build-up in the crater changed the outline of the summit and this can best be seen from the west. A similarly violent eruption with fountaining lava and the ejection of thousands of red-hot projectiles, occurred in 1974-75.

In the last 2000 years the lava flows from Ngauruhoe have been tremendous and you can see them piled up the Mangatepopo Valley.

Pukeonake, a scoria mound, add to the volcanic features of the park. Hauhangatahi is part of an extensive wilderness area west of Ruapehu which offers good walks.

Its winter snow gone, Ngauruhoe reveals from the Mangatepopo Valley the different colours which stamp the passage of time on the cone. The dark course of lava on the right dates from the 1949 and 1954 eruptions, the former being the larger and producing the lower half of the deposit

Tongariro National Park

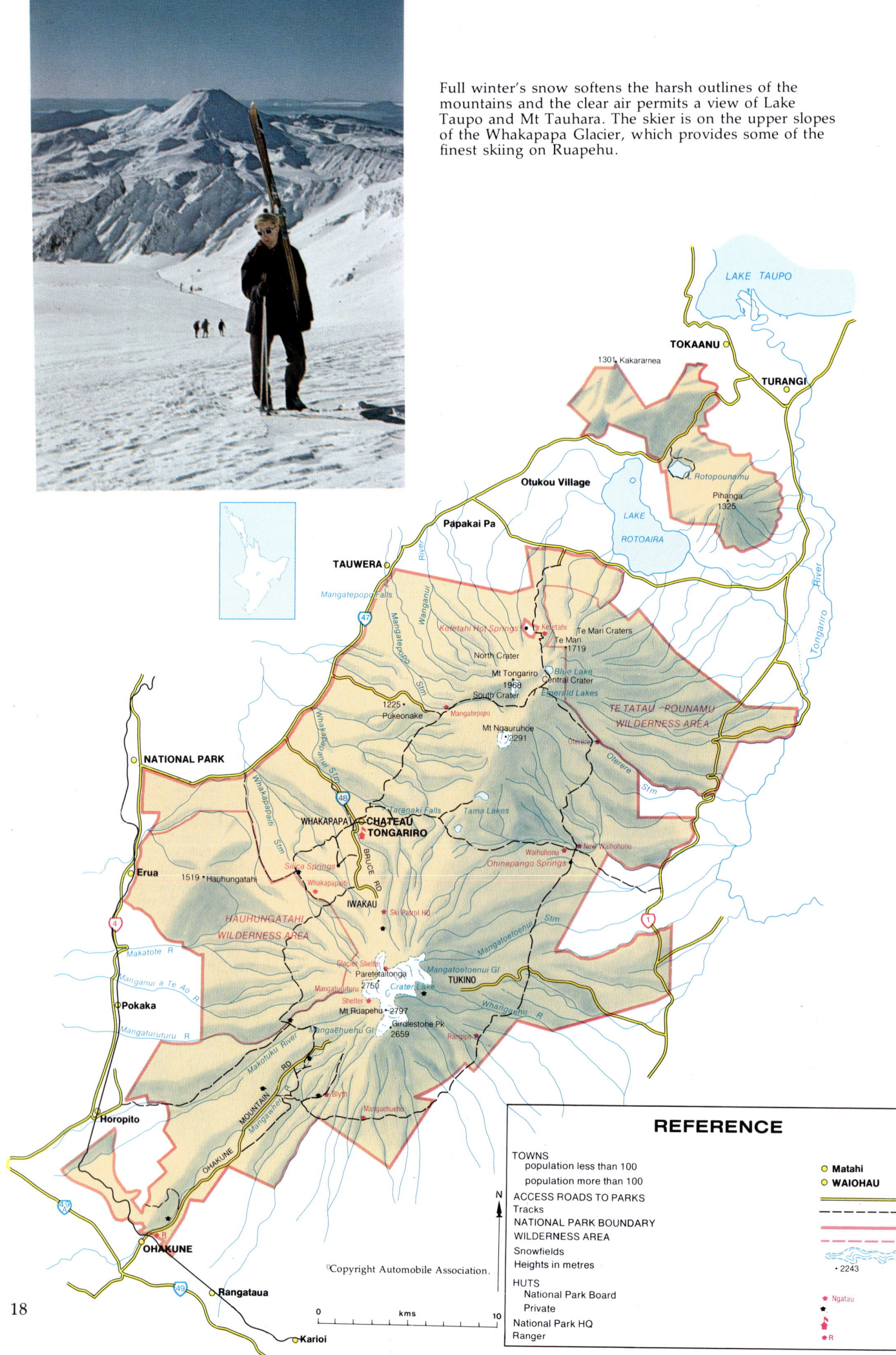

Full winter's snow softens the harsh outlines of the mountains and the clear air permits a view of Lake Taupo and Mt Tauhara. The skier is on the upper slopes of the Whakapapa Glacier, which provides some of the finest skiing on Ruapehu.

©Copyright Automobile Association.

REFERENCE

TOWNS
 population less than 100
 population more than 100
ACCESS ROADS TO PARKS
 Tracks
NATIONAL PARK BOUNDARY
WILDERNESS AREA
 Snowfields
 Heights in metres
HUTS
 National Park Board
 Private
National Park HQ
Ranger

○ Matahi
○ WAIOHAU

· 2243

♠ Ngatau

♠ R

N

0   kms   10

18

There are plenty of short and medium walks within a short distance of the park headquarters. They take you through a divergent landscape of tussock land, mountain beech forest, waterfalls and streams, thermal peculiarities and a range of bird life. Elsewhere in the park are stands of rimu, totara forest, inaka shrubland and red and silver beech forest. If you want to see more of the local birdlife, take a bottle and cork with you into the bush. Rubbing the moistened cork on the bottle will bring the native birds flying to investigate.

Summer is naturally the best time for walking in the park and this is really the season which shows off the diversity of the park, including the minature world of alpine herb fields. In winter the ski slopes of Ruapehu make this New Zealand's most visited national park, but skiers are there for the snow and little else.

They do, though, demonstrate the major issue posed for national parks: how do you provide sufficiently for public access without encouraging access at such a level that the unspoiled nature of the parks is comprised? At Tongariro a great deal of the sense of wilderness has been destroyed by the invasion of ski clubs, ski lifts and similar equipment and the general clutter and traffic which such intensive development inevitably brings.

Recent problems with the development of the Turoa skifields show the paper thin dividing line between use and misuse of a great natural resource. What has happened at Ruapehu does not seem to fit the spirit of the National Parks Act, which speaks of preserving parks as far as possible in their natural state.

Silica Springs are a popular summer attraction. The springs are cold and their water probably comes from much further up the mountain, running down under more recent lava flows and carrying in it silica from volcanic activity high up in the mountain. The creamy rock is coloured by the silica, while the oranges and browns of the Silica Rapids below derive from iron compounds brought by small tributaries from volcanic ash underneath small bogs.

On a high ridge between Ruapehu and Ngauruhoe are Nga Puna-a-Tama (the Springs of Tama), two lakes filling explosion craters. This is the lower of the two.

A fine example of the New Zealand mountain cedar, or kaikawaka (*Libocedrus bidwillii*), on the walk to Silica Springs.

In the beech forest, it is easy to forget that the park is founded on a basement of volcanic lava, although overlying layers of ash provide a bed for the park's plant life.

Tongariro National Park

Fortunate visitors to the park may see the whio, or blue duck, in the more secluded bush streams. Its Maori name comes from the male's distinctive whistling call. The whio is a secretive bird and as the New Zealand bush has retreated from the lowlands into the mountains, the whio has gone with it. It is unique to New Zealand and unique among water fowl, being entirely unrelated to any other species. Unlike other ducks, it feeds not on plants but on water insects, using well-developed claws to scramble over stream boulders and diving with great dexterity.

The size of the major lava flows which have built up the volcanic cones of the park is demonstrated where Taranaki Falls on the Wairere Stream leap more than 20 m over the face of a flow from Ruapehu. Compression at the leading edge of the lava has caused the column-like appearance and the broken rock at the base of the waterfall on the left is a result of the lava's pressure on the ground during its movement.

A snow gentian (*Neopaxia australiasica*)

J. Dryden

To see the park as a whole, you cannot do better than take the 160 km drive around it, taking in the Ohakune mountain road if possible. On the eastern side is the Rangipo desert, created by the deposition of volcanic ash, lava and mud, the rain shadow created by the volcanoes' bulk, the dry winds which funnel between the volcanoes and the Kaimanawa Mountains and the action of frost.

Rangipo (the plains of the dark sky), is named for another example of Ngatotoirangi's ability to influence the gods. He had them send down great black clouds and sleet to destroy a Maori party which was attempting to beat his climb to claim ownership of the volcanoes. The Maori dreaded the desert (one part of it is known as Onetapu, or sacred sands) and those passing through it were not permitted to speak and wore wreaths to shield from their gaze the mountains of the gods.

No wreath would hide the disfiguring power pylons which march gauntly across the desert and which were placed with singular ineptitude between the Desert Road and the mountains.

The cuttings through which the road passes clearly show the layers of ash and carbonised wood laid down over thousands of years. A more recent and continuing disaster is the appearance in the park of pine trees from nearby commercial plantations which are infesting the desert and threatening the survival of the tussock land.

Try to visit Lake Pounamu, a short walk from the saddle road south of Tokaanu. It is a pristine lake where nothing but bush and water are visible. And have a look at the Te Porere redoubt, by State Highway 47, which Te Kooti built for his last stand against his pursuers. Although it is not in the park, it is part of the park's history, for it was Te Kooti's intrusion into the land of the Tuwharetoa which helped to create this national asset.

Tongariro National Park

A rimu among the ferns and other plants of the rain forest on the western side of Ruapehu. In this forest are the few remaining stands of rimu in the park, some of the trees being more than 600 years old and up to 30 m high. The photograph was taken near the Ohakune mountain road, which follows the Mangawhero Stream up to the Turoa skifields.

In the Whakapapaiti Valley the cycle of nature turns from mountain and snow to water and stream, nourishing life below the raw lava slopes of Ruapehu.

Tongariro National Park

The mountain cabbage tree (Cordyline indivisa) bears a much larger head of leaves than the common cabbage tree (C. australis). It is found in upland forests and is particularly common on the Volcanic Plateau.

Urewera National Park

In the beginning were Rangi the sky father and Papa the earth mother. From their union came many children, one of them Tane, the fertiliser of life upon the earth. In his search for the first human mother, Tane created many trees and the birds which lived among and fed on them. They are the children of Tane and the ranges of the Urewera country are their last great stronghold in the North Island of New Zealand.

Urewera National Park is a living shrine to the native forest which once covered the North Island almost without interruption. In it you can sense the spiritual qualities with which the Maori endowed it. They did so because the forest was vital to their existence. They depended on it for food, shelter, tools, canoes and protection and their aim was always to conserve it as much as possible. The forest was consequently under the protection of the gods and tapu for various purposes.

There was a spiritual link, too, between Maori, birds and forest, for all three were descended from Tane and shared a divine ancestry. When you walk through the New Zealand native forest you are walking through the cathedral of the Maori, with rimu, kahikatea, pukatea, kauri and totara for buttress and pillar. In its quietness, broken only by the call of birds or the rush of a stream or waterfall, you can appreciate why the Maori regarded it with reverence.

The native forest of New Zealand has shrunk to a small proportion of its original extent but in Urewera National Park more than 200,000 ha of it is preserved. Here is the home from long ago of the Tuhoe, called Children of the Mist because they are descended from the marriage of Hine-Pukohu-Rangi the Mist Maiden with the mountain, Te Maunga. That metaphor suggests that the origin of the Urewera people is so ancient that it can be only guessed at, being far back beyond the reach of genealogy.

Children of Tane: Forest like this once covered most of New Zealand. Urewera National Park encloses the largest area of it in the North Island.

Myth and legend grew as thickly as the kio-kio in this dense rain forest. In its primeval form before attack by introduced animals, it is so thick that you can scarcely move through it except with the aid of a slasher of some kind. It is easy to imagine spirits and superhuman beings moving though it and among the Maori there grew up a legend of the earliest people in the Urewera forest, a race with unearthly powers. They were the Patu-paiarehe, counterpart of the forest gnomes of the northern hemisphere. They were fair people and were able to spirit the Maori away to their mysterious dens. They could be heard singing eerily when the mist gathered about the hills and valleys. The legend is persuasive when you are tramping among moss-muffled trees in a Urewera mist.

There is uncertainty about the early history of the Maori in the Urewera. But there is no doubt that Urewera National Park retains more than any other a feeling of the rich tradition of its Maori occupation. This was a land fought over for the domination of other tribes rather than for the richness of its living. The Urewera was not hospitable to the Maori with their shortage of warm clothing. Yet the Urewera has much magic and the Maori, sensitive to the spiritual influence of mountain, forest and lake, fully appreciated it.

The Urewera is steep and rugged country and the Huiarau Range which runs through it is part of the backbone of Te Ika-a-Maui, the Fish of Maui – the North Island which Maui hooked and brought up from the depths of the ocean. The ranges lie generally northeast to southwest along the line of the main geological faults which cleave the Urewera. Rivers running along the fault lines have cut deep gorges stepping down through layers of old rock and succeeding pumice and ash from volcanic eruption in the Taupo-Rotorua area. Huge boulders as big as houses litter some of the rivers and waterfalls and cascades abound throughout the park.

Lake Waikaremoana is the scenic centrepiece of Urewera National Park although it is on the southern boundary of an area stretching northwards for almost 70 km. It has had a particularly

The great bluff of Panekire above Waikaremoana.

The Mokau Falls seen from the highway through the park.

vivid place in the history of Tuhoe from the time it was created by the violence of a Taniwha. Long ago at Waikotikoti there lived Maahu-Tapoa-nui, a powerful chief whose name is bestowed on a number of features around the lake. In those days there was no lake, but many rivers and streams winding through the ranges.

One day Maahu asked his daughter, Hau-Mapuhia, to fetch water from a sacred spring, Te Puna-a-Taupara (the Spring of Taupara). She refused and Maahu went in a rage to the well himself. He brooded over his daughter's disobedience and his anger had not abated when Hau-Mapuhia arrived at the well to see what was delaying her father. Maahu seized her and thrust her head into the water of the spring to drown her. Hau-Mapuhia struggled to escape and called out to ancient Maori gods, who took pity on her and turned her into a Taniwha, a huge water spirit in dragon-like form. She tore herself from her father's grasp and grew immense, too large for any river. In her struggle to escape to the sea she threw herself about, carving out first one then another great gouge in the earth.

The waters of rivers and streams rushed to fill these furrows, forming the arms and inlets of a lake. Hau-Mapuhia's thrashing about so whipped up the water that it became known as Waikaremoana – the Sea of Dashing Waters. Hau-Mapuhia could not break through the high ranges which encircle the lake and was caught by the rising sun and turned to stone in the gorge of the Waikaretaheke River just below Kaitawa, where the power scheme now harnesses the water. For ages she lay there for people to see but since the hydro-electric project a landslip has covered her. Mark her grave with respect for she left us a beautiful lake in a spectacular setting. Listen for her voice which still echoes over the Huiarau Range when the westerly gales blow.

Of course the white man with his science found a different and less rhapsodical way of explaining the origin of the lake. Several thousand years ago, a landslide blocked the valley between the Panekire and Ngamoko Ranges. The slip was about 8 km long and 4 km wide and the road from Wairoa crosses it at the entrance to the park by Onepoto. It moved about 1.5 km from the Ngamoko Range and even today it is extremely broken ground, with caves and fissures, sudden hilly outcrops up to 30 m high and big rocks splaying out of the ground like giant tombstones in a derelict graveyard. Through it now pass the tunnels feeding water to the power scheme.

The power development has changed the natural outflow of water from Lake Waikaremoana. It is estimated that the lake rose very slowly behind the natural dam formed by the slip, the voids of which became the first outlet for the lake waters. They emerged about 200 m below the top of the landslide as springs discharging some 14 cubic metres a second to form the source of the Waikaretaheke River. These underground outlets were called Te Whangaromanga (bay of disappearing) and above them was a whirlpool in the lake. Only when the lake was at its fullest level would it overflow at its surface outlet, Te Wharawhara, a narrow and shallow channel over the top of the slip above the springs. This was dry about 50% of the time and today its flat, terraced beds of rock are permanently dry.

There were Maori in the Urewera long before Hau-Mapuhia made Lake Waikaremoana. Tuhoe held the land north and west of the lake and were a small tribe, independent and isolated from the tribes which lived in others parts of the Urewera country. They were apparently able for a long time to stay aloof from the seesaw of victory and defeat which characterised the fierce life of the other tribes. The first of these is said to have been Ngai Tauira. They were defeated by Ngati Kahungunu in a major battle known as Taupara at a place near Frasertown and only sketchy knowledge of them has survived – Maori oral tradition had no room for memorials to the defeated.

Ngai Tauira are remembered, though, in the name of the strait which separates the main body of Lake Waikaremoana from the arm called Wairaumoana, named for its deep blue colour which is likened to a bruise. The strait is called Te Kaunga-o-Manaia (the Swimming of Manaia) because of the Tauira chief who first swam it. There is a very old pa site on the southern shore of the strait called Nga Whatu-a-Tama (the Eyes of Tama) after another Tauira chief. From there a watch could be kept on the narrow water. It is a small bush-covered mound at the entrance to the strait.

Ngati Ruapani were a dominant tribe after the dispersal of Ngai Tauira and are still represented by people living at Waikaremoana. It was they who in more recent times became gradually involved in conflict with Tuhoe, conflict which became more savage as it proceeded. Tuhoe were a proud people and none in or about the Urewera had an older claim to their land. They were descended from Tuhoe Potiki, himself claimed to be a descendant of the renowned Toi-Kai-Rakau (Toi Whose Food Came from the Trees), a name which reflects the importance of berries and birds to the Maori. Toi is said to have had a pa by the Whakatane River a long time before the Great Migration of the Maori by canoe from their ancestral homeland about 1350. The people of Toi had spread widely over the land by then.

Maahu-Tapoa-nui is believed by some to have descended from Toi. Whether he did or not, he left his name prominently around the shores of Waikaremoana. By Te Ure-o-Patae Island in Wairaumoana is a point called Nga Whanau-a-Maahu (the Family of Maahu), after a group of stones into which Maahu's other children were turned because they had desecrated the sacred well, Te Puna-a-Taupara. So strong was the tapu placed on this stream that it is said birds flying over it would drop dead from the sky. Near his old pa in Te Pa-a-Maahu Bay is a small pond Te Wai Whakaata-a-Maahu (the Mirror of Maahu) and opposite this across the lake is Te Whata-Kai-a-Maahu (the Food Storehouse of Maahu), a small island of rock where he kept food safe from marauders – two and four legged.

Beware of the flax plants which grow on the cliff by Nga Whanau-a-Maahu – they are Nga Makawe-o-Maahu (the Hair of Maahu) and if you touch them there will be cast on you a spell which will prevent you from leaving the lake.

The great navigator Kupe, perhaps the first Polynesian to discover New Zealand, is said to have visited Waikaremoana. Just off the Te Ahititi cliffs, a little way inside the park on the road from Wairoa, are Nga Hoe-o-Kupe (the Paddles of Kupe), rocks of vertical strata which had the power to change the direction of the wind when struck.

One of the canoes of the Great Migration which came after Kupe was the Mataatua, which made landfall at Whakatane and whose people spread into the Urewera country, intermarrying with those who had come before them. It seems that as a result of this intermingling, the original inhabitants of the Urewera chose to call themselves Tuhoe to distinguish themselves from the later arrivals and the name gradually became a regional one. The captain of the Mataatua canoe was Toroa and his descendants intermarried with those of Toi, Tuhoe Potiki being one of the subsequent progeny. The name of Urewera came from an accident to this son, Mura Kareke, who was lying by a fire in his old age when he rolled into it and suffered a burn (wera) to his genitals which proved fatal. The name was given with Maori drollery to the district in which Mura's clan lived.

Some Maori historians say that the more warlike Maori of the Great Migration infused warrior blood into Tuhoe and that as time passed they became more aggressive. That may be, but Ruapani sparked off a long war in the ranges when in about 1660 they crossed the Huiarau Range, a natural southern boundary of Tuhoe, and attacked the latter at Ruatahuna. Tuhoe returned the visit and had a great victory at Hopuruahine (literally, to Seize the Old Woman, a reference to another Taniwha incident). Ruapani made a desperate further stand near Te Ana-Putaputa Cave, where a narrow beach is backed by a steep cliff. Their blood stained the sand red.

This victory helped to persuade Tuhoe that they had a place around the lake as well as in their long-held territory northwest of the Huiarau Range. They began to settle there in increasing numbers and this led to further friction with

A large northern rata grips the trunk of an old tree which has played host to it since its life began as a small perching plant.

neighbouring tribes. The usual pattern of insult, raid, battle and, as always, utu – the principle of evening or 'wiping off' a score – followed but eventually peace was made between Tuhoe and Ruapani and lasted until the early 19th Century. Then Ruapani apparently murdered two Tuhoe chiefs staying at Hopuruahine and mutilated the body of one of them. For some time it was carried about as a kind of one-man circus attraction which was locally popular. Tuhoe came over the ranges in a huge party to avenge this enormous insult and fought a big battle with Ruapani at Whakairi Pa, one of the most famous pa of Lake Waikaremoana.

This pa is on a small point in Paraeroa Bay. It fell to the Tuhoe warriors and Ruapani fled across the Whanganui inlet of the lake to Pukehuia Pa. They took all their canoes with them except for those they had sunk when hearing of the Tuhoe war party's approach. So intent on utu were the Tuhoe men that they immediately set about building two canoes. They called one Roimata-nui (Many Tears) and the other Ruha-nui (Great Weariness), both names presumably reflecting the arduous nature of the undertaking. In these canoes they attacked Pukehuia and inflicted terrible slaughter.

The war sputtered on for half a century, one of its most grisly episodes being the massacre of defenceless Tuhoe women, children and old men in Te Ana-a-Tikitiki (the Cave of Tikitiki), which is near the lake shore in Otekuri Bay. The cave was filled with corpses and many of them were thrown into the lake. A nearby point subsequently became known as Te Wai Kotero because the stench of bodies resembled that of decaying potatoes. The event is still remembered with profound feeling by Tuhoe people and the cave still has a grim air as though the spirit of death lingers there yet. The following reprisal by Tuhoe warriors drove Ruapani from their strongholds around the lake and although they tried later with the help of Kahungunu to recover their land, they failed to oust Tuhoe. All agreed on peace in 1863.

The forest fastness of the Urewera offered perfect ground for the guerilla tactics of the Maori who fought the pakeha over land in the 19th Century. To it came Te Kooti during his long conflict with Government forces – Te Kooti, the Maori whom white settlers most feared and hated because of his mana, his savagery and his tactical abilities. Here in the Urewera the hostilities between a tiring Te Kooti and his men and the Government forces ebbed away to signal the end of New Zealand's land wars.

The Maori of the Urewera at first welcomed white men and proved as hospitable as they were to the first Europeans throughout New Zealand. William Colenso, missionary, explorer and botanist, found them so when he visited them in 1841 but 20 years later the pakeha was no longer welcome: The Urewera had turned completely against the Government. That is an uncomfortable reflection of the Maori sense of betrayal and loss over the land question. Urewera tribes fought minor battles around Wairoa in the 1860s as the tide of Maori resistance rose and the first Government foray into the high ranges came in 1866, when Major Fraser led a force including Maori allies to victory at Tuai. Some 400 anti-Government Maori were shot to death after their capture.

In 1865 the fanatical Hauhau belief reached the East Coast of the North Island and the war intensified, with a fierce battle at Waerenga-a-Hika near Turanga, now Gisborne. One of those who fought with the Government forces was Te Kooti, who was accused of being a spy and, in somewhat suspicious circumstances (it has been claimed that he was the victim of conspiracy), deported with other prisoners to the Chatham Islands for detention in 1866. There he became known as a prophet, subject to visions, capable of miracles (or frauds?) and fond of leading his fellow-prisoners in prayer. Then in 1868 he led them to escape by organising the overthrow of the guards, taking the schooner *Rifleman* and commanding its captain to sail to Gisborne. One death occurred in the uprising and the official report remarked on Te Kooti's moderation and the absence of looting.

Landing near Gisborne, Te Kooti headed for Te Whaiti, harassed by settlers and soldiers, possibly seeking only to avoid fighting and to use the Urewera to keep his distance from the European. However, in November of 1868 he returned to the coast in a surprise raid and massacred 29 pakeha and 32 Maori at Matawhero. This set the country alight and a running battle developed, Te Kooti unable to stand and fight against superior firepower, losing two pitched battles at Ngatapa, Poverty Bay, and Te Porere, Taupo, but dictating the running fight tactics. The forbidding Urewera and Tuhoe were two of his main strengths. The Armed Constabulary and its Maori allies spent from 1869 to 1872 pursuing Te Kooti through the Urewera, burning villages and destroying crops as they went in the kind of campaign familiar in modern times. Some 200 Maori in Ruatahuna alone are estimated to have died from consequent starvation and exposure. In April, 1871, Tuhoe gave up their struggle and made peace with the Government. Te Kooti eventually escaped to the King Country and the Government in turn gave up, pardoning him in 1883.

The kakariki, or yellow-crowned parrot is moderately common in the park, having once been widespread throughout native forest at all altitudes. Its survival in the heavy bush of the Urewera is a symbol of the protective capacities of untouched native forest.

The mournful cry of the forest which signals evening comes from the morepork, or ruru. At dusk it begins its hunt from a prominent perch for insects. It is one of the two owls native to New Zealand.

G. Moon

WAIKIRIKIRI   Tanatana

795
Raroa

765·
Te Whakaumu   Whakarae

Waihua Stm

Ohora
Ohora Stm   Kaharoa
792· Koaunui   1025
926·   R   Tawai
Hikurangi
832·   767·
Rakautapu   890·
Okopeka

670·
GALATEA   Orangitutaetutu   1315·
Ngapuketurua
Mangawhero   849·
Forks   Kanohinui   900·
1017·   Te Rangaaruanuku   882·
MURUPARA   Tawhiuau   Pawairoto   Te Rangiakapua·
R   1350·
Tarakena
Rapids
Tawhiwhi   Makomako·
Ariki Tuhoe Cliffs
·975   1366·
1037·
Te Whaiti   Whakaipu

Okaura Stm

RUATAHUNA   38

Shelter

Kopuapounamu Stm
Tauwhare
Falls
·1402
Manueha· Manuoha
Silted Lake Bed
1262·   Sandy Bay
Whakataka
Pakura Bluff   Cascades   Lake
852·   Shelter   Walkareiti
Whanganui   1055·
Aniwaniwa
Falls   Papakorito Falls
Te Puna   Aniwaniwa
Hot   928·   Waikaremoana
Springs   Marauiti
LAKE   1101·
WAIKAREMOANA   Ngamoko   N
Kokooro   Panekiri
Falls   Bluff
1269·   Waiopaoa   Panekiri· Puketapu   Redoubt
1180·   TUAI

0   kms   10

31

In the park headquarters museum at Aniwaniwa are the remains of two boats which one abortive European expedition built to give themselves aquatic mobility but which they sank in Lake Waikaremoana when recalled by a nervous Government. Another sign of the conflict is the grave at Lake Kiri-o-Pukae of Trooper Michael Noonan, ambushed while carrying despatches. Te Kooti had a pa with a finely-carved meeting house at Matuahu on the lake. Remnants of an Armed Constabulary redoubt survive at Onepoto, by the southern road entrance to the park. Te Ana-a-Moko (Cave of the Moko) is named for an occasion when Te Kooti stopped to rest and several women followers received the moko (tattoo).

There is a link between Te Kooti and another Maori who made a significant impression on the Urewera – Rua Kenana, born in 1869 after his father, Kenana Tumoana, was killed at Makaretu while fighting for Te Kooti during his withdrawal inland from the Matawhero massacre. Kenana Tumoana was a high-born member of Tuhoe, descended from Potiki and Toroa. Rua learned farming in Poverty Bay, studied the Bible and in 1905 moved to Maungapohatu as a New Testament prophet. He claimed divinity and followers vested land in him. He established a special Parliament to administer the settlement and developed a community which gave Tuhoe a prosperity they had never before enjoyed. He acted as a patriarch, promoted the idea of Maoridom as a separate community within New Zealand and earned the jealousy of rivals and the enmity of the Government. Tuhoe came close to internecine war because of his influence. Liquor offences, perhaps used as a pretext for confining someone who argued that the Maori should boycott World War 1 military service, put Rua in prison in 1916 after a gun battle with police, in which two Maori were killed, one of them Rua's son, and several police were wounded. By the time of his release, his mana was destroyed and his movement dwindled away. His was the last flourish against established power by the proud people of the Urewera.

The history of the Maori in the Urewera breathes through the leaves of the trees and sounds in the lap of lake and rush of stream and waterfall. It can be caught by visitors who read the old tales and identify the places where they were acted out.

The brooding spirit of the Urewera ranges and their identification with Maori mettle may have been a reason for pakeha pressure which after World War 1 sought to have the Urewera subdivided into farms and its bush cleared. Did the pakeha in the Bay of Plenty see in the massed bush and skyline of the Urewera ranges the old power of the Maori? Fears of erosion on the steep hills denuded of forest and doubts about farming profitability on the soil proved more persuasive in the end and the theme of forest protection took firmer root as time passed. It was in some ways a miracle that the Urewera forest survived the onslaught which elsewhere in the North Island raised blackened tree stumps as monuments to economic desire. The park was established in 1954 and now has an area of more than 210,000 ha, making it New Zealand's third largest. The Maori tribes lease the bed of the lake to the Park Board.

The sleek, plump New Zealand pigeon was a favourite food of the Maori, who used to snare it at drinking troughs used by the bird after feeding on berries.

R. Van de Voort

The bush is the glory of the park, clothing it in a continuous garment which has no equivalent in our other national parks. It is impossible not to sense the regard of the Maori for it, as Elsdon Best demonstrated in his book 'Forest Lore of the Maori'. In it he quotes an old Maori as saying about the time Te Kooti disappeared into the King Country: 'Our forests were to us a rich possession, such trees as the totara, miro, matai, rimu, rata, maire, tawa, kahikatea, karaka, hinau and others, were invaluable to us as they provided both bird and man with food and also man with materials wherefrom were fashioned canoes, houses, defensive stockades and a great variety of implements. So it was that care was taken to prevent the damage of forests by fire, lest such valuable trees be destroyed.' He bewailed the reduction in bird numbers through the European's introduction of animals and the burning of forest. The Maori spoke very carefully to Tane before felling a great tree and often made tapu an area of large canoe building. There were many rules governing their relations with the gods and spirits of the forest.

Nowhere is the interdependence of plant communities better illustrated than in the New Zealand rain forest. Its richness cannot be matched by exotic forests.

The kowhai is unusual in being one of New Zealand's few deciduous native trees and its beautiful yellow bloom has been adopted as the national flower.

The forest of Urewera National Park allows us to see the past today.

The solitude of Waikaremoana.

The forest covers all of the ridges so that high views are of uninterrupted vegetation. Rimu, rata and tawa are the important trees at the lower levels, with rimu and beech dominant up to 900 m, when red and silver beech, with some mountain beech in a few uppermost places, become the park's crowning vegetation. There is a rimu-rata association as at Egmont National Park. Matai and totara grow among the rimu in various places and kohekohe is well represented in the eastern part of the park. The buttress-trunked pukatea and the mangaeo are common and the miro grows here to remind us of the bonds between bird and tree – its berries are a favourite of the fat New Zealand pigeon. Perching and climbing plants abound and the New Zealand ferns, mosses and lichens, a multitude as rich in variety as anywhere on earth, are at their best. The track to Mt Manuoha (1403 m), the highest point in the park, passes through a wonderfully green world of "moss forest" and ends at the park's only alpine grassland, just a few hectares in area, and sub-alpine scrub which is also found on Mt Maungapohatu (1366 m).

Although deer and opossum have wreaked their usual damage in the forest, it still supports a profuse variety of native birds, supplemented by exotic species. A kiwi may show itself in your headlights at night, and you will hear its whistle on summer evenings, the largest specimens of kahu , or harrier hawk, frequent the highway and you may sight the toutouwai, or North Island robin, which is now uncommon but still found here. The pigeon, one of the Maori's favourite foods, which was trapped by snare while drinking from troughs placed in trees whose berries, particularly the miro, formed its diet, is plentiful. The piopio, or native North Island thrush, may still survive here. Some people hold out hope that the huia, that unique bird, may be alive yet in the Urewera but the evidence seems against it. Its rediscovery would be a sensation. Its feathers were used as decoration by the highest chiefs and the male and female had differently shaped beaks, the male a short one for hacking at the wood of fallen trees, the female a long, slender, curved one for pulling out grubs. The name of the Huiarau Range means many huia.

A warning against thoughtless development around New Zealand's most scenic areas is the lowering of the lake level for hydro-electric purposes. Three power stations in series below the outlet of Lake Waikaremoana cause fluctuations in the lake level and although the original bush has not been drowned, there is an unsightly and intrusive gap of naked shore between water and trees.

Walking and tramping through the packed beauty of New Zealand native forest is available in immense variety in Urewera National Park. Streams, rivers and waterfalls thread the dark bush with light. Lakes Waikaremoana and

Waikareiti (Little Dashing Water) shine their individual and changing moods on the country about them. A four-day tramp around Lake Waikaremoana from Onepoto (Short Beach) to Hopuruahine by the western shore follows a well-made track constructed over 10 years by schoolboy parties. It is an excellent way of seeing the variety of the park.

Lake Waikareiti is only a 3.5 km walk from the highway and should be included on any visit to the park, for it is untouched and lies serenely between bush dropping to the water's edge. There are six small islands in the lake, one of which, Rahui, has a tiny lake, Te Tamaiti-o-Waikaremoana (the Child of Waikaremoana). Waikareiti used to be used as a refuge by Ruapani in troubled times. An alternative route to it passes by two small lakes and there is a track around Waikareiti itself, with an extension to the old silted lake bed of Kaipo Lagoon.

The outlet of Waikareiti is Aniwaniwa Stream, on which the Papakorito Falls lie only a short distance from the highway. This is one of several beautiful falls and cascades in the park.

A highway bridge makes only the barest impression on the bush and water wilderness of the Urewera.

The Hopuruahine Cascades are among the finest in New Zealand, dropping down between monstrous rocks. The Mokau and Aniwaniwa Falls are exceedingly beautiful.

There are several main tracks through the park – from Maungapohatu down the Tauranga and Waimana Rivers to State Highway 2, from Ruatahuna down the Whakatane River to Ruatoki North and from the southern sector of the park across the eastern boundary into western Poverty Bay.

Urewera National Park is large, much larger than it appears to the casual visitor who traverses it by road and tends to identify it with the environs of Waikaremoana. It is a park which allows you to steep yourself with relative ease in the vaulted grandeur of the native forest which once cloaked Te Ika-a-Maui. And which holds in its embrace the legends, traditions and old ways of the Maori.

National Publicity Studios

Mighty rocks guide the Hopuruahine Cascades down towards Lake Waikaremoana.

35

Egmont National Park

Time's slow march has made a volcanic stairway across the face of Taranaki.

The stairway rises in giant steps from the ocean's edge to end at Mt Egmont, that most distinctive of New Zealand mountains.

Mt Egmont stands sharp and proud above the plains of Taranaki. It is one of the world's most striking shapes and perhaps our most famous landmark.

Egmont's beauty and symmetry ensures its fame yet the park named after it encloses two other major volcanoes. Their presence is subdued against the magnificence of Egmont but they are very much part of the story of volcanic birth and decay which has culminated in Egmont.

Before Egmont came Pouakai and before Pouakai came Kaitake. Together they are a three-step demonstration of the eternal battle between mountain building and the elements. It is a battle which wind and water must win and Kaitake and Pouakai show in their eroded forms how long the battle has been in progress. It continues, and Egmont too is on its way to a similar fate.

Egmont is the most recent of a series of ruptures which over tens of thousands of years spread southeast along a line of weakness in the earth's crust. Had all of them occurred within just a few thousand years of each other, we would now see three similar volcanic peaks in a line no more than 17 km long.

Weathering has lost us this sight but instead we have in the park a unique display of nature destroying slowly what it has built. It graphically illustrates the fluid nature of our planet.

For the earth is always changing. Our individual lives are so brief that the landscape seems to us to be relatively stable. Nevertheless we can see telltale signs of change around us – boulders littering a stream, the breaking of ice from

Old lava flows stand out clearly on Mt Egmont, solidified records of a violent past. Nature's constant worrying of high mountains shows in the boulders and water of Kapuni Stream. Here native bush flourishes, but up on the mountain's higher slopes, sub-alpine scrub has a harder struggle to survive.

The most prominent of the two oldest volcanic cones in Egmont National Park is Pouakai, its lava slopes showing a strong resemblence to those of Mt Egmont but its former cone truncated by erosion.

National Publicity Studios

Lyric Studio

Centuries of rain and melting snow have patterned Mt Egmont with radiating furrows cut through volcanic rock. Down them flows the mountain's gift of water to the Taranaki plains below. Fanthams Peak is on the left.

Summer bares the slopes of Mt Egmont but even high temperatures on the lava cannot prevent tenacious plant life from maintaining its grip. Below the summit, alpine herbfields and fellfields wrap a light-coloured band around the mountain sides. Sub-alpine scrub like that in the foreground growing on Pouakai gives Egmont a lower, dark-green girdle.

glaciers, hillside erosion, the pattern of rockforms along a shoreline. Nothing remains the same.

The building of the heights on which Egmont National Park is founded started perhaps 600,000 years ago, when the earliest known men were beginning to appear on earth. Certainly the first of the Taranaki volcanoes, Kaitake, was active 575,000 years ago. It probably rose to rather less than the height of Egmont today but climate, that great leveller, has reduced it to a series of radiating ridges no higher than 684 m, compared with Egmont's 2518 m. A once prominent peak has become simply the Kaitake Range and from the ground its volcanic origins are not clear. From the air, though, its original nature is evident.

As Kaitake's activity slowly diminished, the volcanic building of the land continued with Pouakai, 10 km to the southeast. It was active about 250,000 years ago and spewed out sufficient material to form a ringplain equivalent to the modern one built by Egmont. Pouakai spread ash over a great area of Taranaki and at New Plymouth there is a layer of it some 30 m thick.

Pouakai, too, was a major volcano but it has now eroded to a peak height of 1399 m and a diameter of between two thirds and a half that of the Egmont cone.

The ringplain built by Pouakai is, like Egmont's, a classic example of the way debris fans out from the volcanic centre, carried by collapses of main crater walls, the release of crater lakes, heavy rainfall or general erosion leading to landslides. An avalanche of rock, scoria, ash and, usually, water which result from this natural attrition is called by the Indonesian name lahar. Lahars are a constant part of volcanic activity and they can be huge and extremely destructive.

In western Taranaki there are thousands of small mounds which were formed by lahar deposits.

J. Drydon

Green farmland sweeps up to the dark bush which marks the boundary of Egmont National Park, a contrast between pastoral development and forest conservation. Above stands one of New Zealand's exceptional landmarks, with Fanthams Peak the only interruption to the mountain's profile.

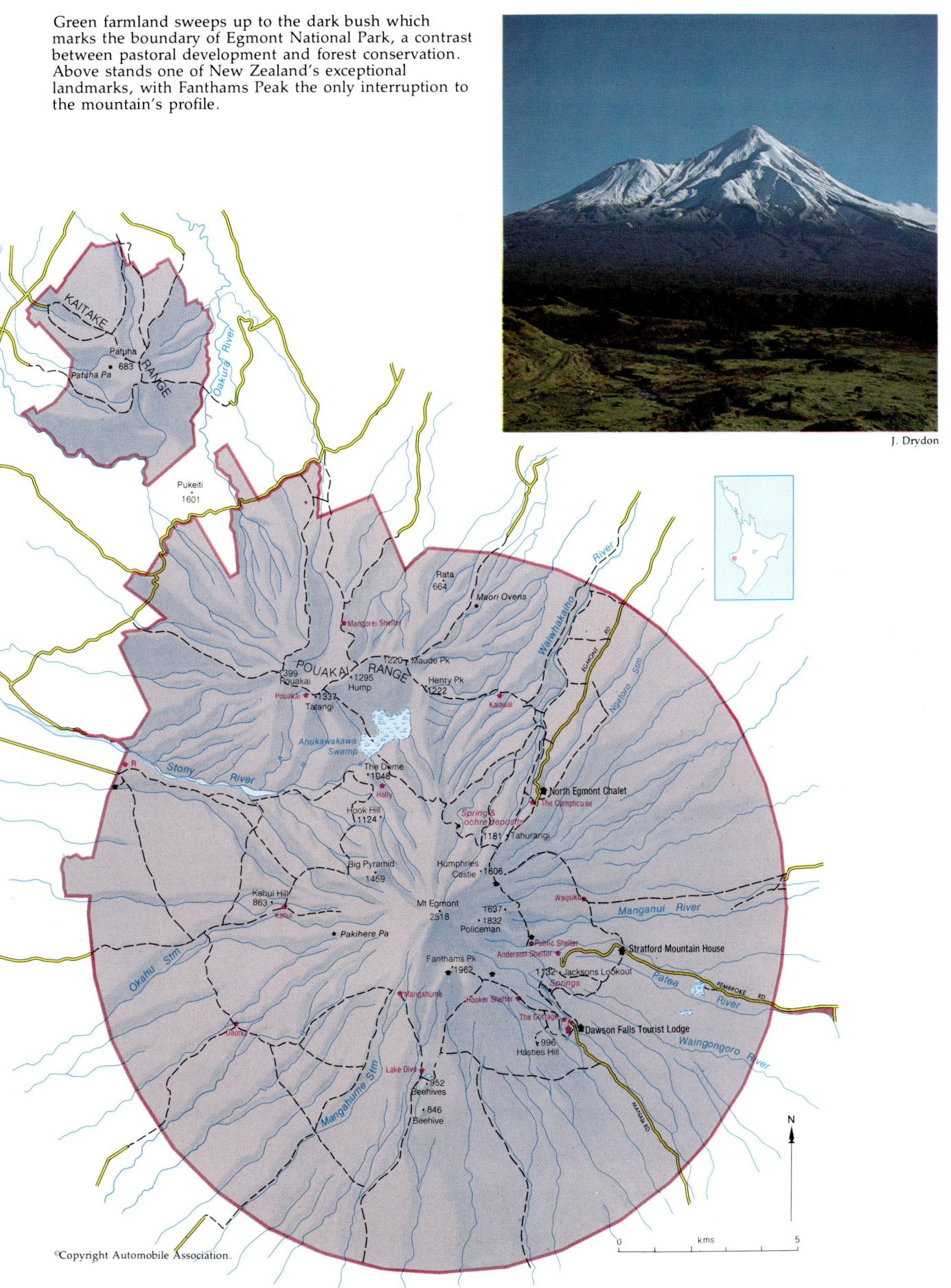

J. Drydon

KAITAKE RANGE

Oakura River

Patuha
• 683
Patuha Pa

Pukeiti
• 1601

Rata
664

Maori Ovens

• Mangorei Shelter

Waiwhakaiho River

POUAKAI RANGE

• 399
Pouakai

1220 • Maude Pk

• 1295
Hump

Henry Pk
1222

EGMONT RD

• Pouakai • 1337
Tatangi

• Kaiauai

Ngatoro Stm

Ahukawakawa Swamp

Stony   River

R

The Dome
• 1048

• Holly

North Egmont Chalet
The Camphouse

Hook Hill
1124

Springs
ochre Deposits

Big Pyramid
1459

• 1181 Tahurangi

Humphries Castle • 1606

Kahui Hill
863 •

• Kahui

Mt Egmont
2518

• 1637
• 1832
Policeman

Waipuke

Manganui River

• Pakihere Pa

Public Shelter
Anderson Shelter •

Stratford Mountain House

Okahu Stm

Fanthams Pk
• 1962

1132 • Jacksons Lookout
Springs

Patea River

PEMBROKE RD

• Mangahume

Hooker Shelter

The Cottage

Dawson Falls Tourist Lodge

• 996
Hasties Hill

Waingongoro River

• Uaunu

Mangahume Stm

Lake Dive

• 952
Beehives

MANAIA RD

• 846
Beehive

N

0   kms   5

©Copyright Automobile Association.

The Pouakai ringplain spread out to the coast and large parts of it are still well preserved along a line between Okato and Inglewood and along the eastern boundary of the subsequent Egmont ringplain. In these areas, the nature of the land provided protection against the flow of later, devastating lahars from Egmont, just as big boulders will part the flow of a river.

Pouakai was probably much the same height as Egmont and the last Ice Age, which ended about 14,000 years ago, helped to reduce it to its present shape. Since then, volcanic ash from Egmont has softened its outlines and helped to create the peculiar, finger-like shapes spreading out from the Pouakai range at its lower levels. Their volcanic origin is best revealed from the air.

Egmont is thought to have appeared by 70,000 years ago. The coastal cliffs of Taranaki preserve many lahar deposits which date from about that time. Most of the southern Pouakai ringplain has been overlaid by the outpour from Egmont. The mountain is believed to have grown to its present size, but with two peaks, by about 35,000 years ago and from then until some 25,000 years ago, there was frequent activity which sent many lahars charging down to the west or southeast. They are now deeply buried by subsequent eruption.

At about the end of this period came one of the most dramatic events in Egmont's life. Most of the northern crater, which was slightly to the west of the present summit, collapsed and the whole upper part of the cone went sliding west as a monstrous lahar. It travelled to beyond the present coastline, a distance of more than 30 km. One of the mightiest lahars ever, it covered about 200 sq km with material at least 30 m thick.

There have been two other events of similar magnitude, one covering about 300 sq km in the Okato, Oaonui and Kaponga districts and the other spreading over 120 sq km in the Opunake area. They were major factors in the creation of today's Taranaki landscape.

About 20,000 years ago, Egmont was building its present cone and from then until quite recently – in geological terms – the mountain was spilling over lava to form the series of lava cliffs and gorges which are apparent today. During this period the mountain was throwing out the ash which provides Taranaki farming pastures with their topsoil.

An early part of this activity was the formation of another small cone, Pukeiti, between Kaitake and Pouakai.

The most recent main phase, which took place over the last few thousand years, included the building of Fanthams Peak on the side of Egmont's main cone. It was named after Fanny Fantham, who in 1871, at the age of 19, became the first woman to reach the top. The peak is 1962 m high.

Other activity during this time was the extrusion of lava which formed the distinctive Dome, the two Beehives and Skinner Hill. They are great rounded lumps shaped by the relatively rapid cooling of lava which was not ejected with sufficient force or volume to disperse it. Instead, it welled up and cooled over its vents.

Volcanic activity from Egmont was still going on after the Maori settled in the district and Cook missed seeing it in action by only a few years. There was an eruption around 1655, just 13 years after Tasman arrived at New Zealand although he did not see the mountain. This eruption showered ash over the southeast sector of the park and you can still see the effects of it today in the buried bases of trees which survived the eruption. At about the same time lava erupted in the crater to form the present tholoid, or lava plug. This activity was not large by previous Egmont standards and the last eruption in about 1755 was small, spreading ash only over the upper part of the mountain.

Kapuni Stream pauses briefly in the stepped series of Wilkies Pools, named for two farmer brothers prominent in early climbing days on Egmont. Water and its cargo of rock and gravel have cut down through lava thousands of years old. A beautiful nature walk from Dawsons Falls up to the pool follows the stream's tumbling path through bush.

The volcanic history of Egmont shows itself in a bank where Kapuni Stream has sliced down through successive ash layers.

It is too soon yet to regard Egmont as extinct, although it is often referred to as such.

During the last 35,000 years, it has been erosion rather than volcanic action which has influenced the shape of the Taranaki ringplains. Flows of volcanic debris in lahars, most often caused by heavy rain, have had substantial impacts on vegetation, topography and river and stream patterns.

The Maori legend of Taranaki moving to its present position from the central volcanic plateau is told in the chapter on Tongariro National Park but the surprising thing about a mountain as visually dominant as Egmont is that there is no other Maori tradition associated with the mountain. That legend came from the Maori at Tongariro and those who lived in Taranaki as long ago as 1000 A.D. established no known local lore.

Both Cook in 1770 and later the Frenchman Marion du Fresne, saw Maori fires on shore. There is little evidence around the mountain of Maori occupation.

Two Maori ovens discovered in the early 1930s and in 1972 only deepen this mystery. One was found near the Stratford Mountain House on the eastern side of the mountain and the other on a tributary of the Waingongoro River. They are well up the mountain in the sub-alpine scrub zone, where the Maori would have been unlikely to have lived or even have visited often, as the forest below provided his larder.

Possible religious significance has been ascribed to the presence of these ovens but this seems unlikely in the absence of associated Maori legend or tradition. Perhaps the ovens were used when local tribes retreated from enemy marauders, as they did in the Kahui Gorge up on the mountain side.

The higher slopes of the mountain were tapu. The Maori used to gather red ochre from the mountain's gorges for pigment which was important to their art and buildings and they used caves and crevices as the resting place of the bones of chiefs and tohungas, or high priests.

From the historical point of view it is unfortunate that Cook, sailing with all the assurance of one whose nation ruled the seas, should have so freely tossed names at New Zealand landmarks. Unaware of the Maori legend which so imaginatively links the name of Taranaki with the fabled volcanoes in the centre of the North Island, he named the mountain after the Earl of Egmont, First Lord of the Admiralty.

The Maori name is surely more appropriate than that of a forgotten British sealord, but the European residents of the province did not see it that way when they objected a few years ago to a proposal to officially restore the original name.

The first ascent of the mountain by Europeans was made in 1839 by the naturalist with the New Zealand Company, Ernst Dieffenbach, and a whaler, James Heberley. During the 1860s and

1870s, summer ascents of Egmont were popular and a track was established across the Pouakai Ranges. To their eternal credit, the people of Taranaki early recognised the need to protect Egmont and its forest and a large area was vested in the Provincial Council. In 1881 the land within a six-mile (9.6 km) radius of the summit was reserved under the Land Act for the "growth and preservation of timber". In 1900, after the Kaitake Range had been included in the reserve, Parliament passed legislation which established Egmont National Park.

There are now 33,530 ha in the park. There is an unfortunate gap between the Egmont-Pouakai boundary and the Kaitake Range boundary, although the small cone of Pukeiti is islanded between the two main park areas. The Pukeiti Rhododendron Trust makes an incongrous, foreign intrusion into this gap.

Egmont's ascendancy over the surrounding country has effects which are not merely visual. In many ways, the mountain has the characteristics of an island, separated not by water but by height and climate. It is remarkable for the absence of mountain beech, which is common to other New Zealand mountains and is found in profusion on Ruapehu, only 130 km away. More than 100 common species of native vegetation which you would expect to find on Egmont and Pouakai are absent.

Another peculiar aspect of this separation from general evolution is that Egmont has varieties of common plants – broom, koromiko, tussock grass, harebell, mountain daisy and ourisia – which are not found elsewhere in New Zealand.

The same thing has happened with insects, many of which have evolved differently from their counterparts elsewhere, including those found only as far away as Ruapehu. The absence of mountain beech has helped to promote these evolutionary diversions. Egmont has two rare Hepialid moths, Aoraia leonina and the smaller Dioxycanus oreas. There is an extraordinary association between the larvae of these species and one of the local plants. The larvae feed underground and their diet renders them liable to be taken over by the fungus Cordiceps robertsii. The fungus grows within the larva's living body and gradually kills it. The fungus turns woody in the shape of the unfortunate caterpillar and from its erstwhile host sends up its fruiting body.

There is an excellent introduction to the stick insects, moths, wetas, millipedes and beetles in the attractive visitors' centre at the top of the Dawson Falls road.

High rainfall on Mt Egmont creates many waterfalls and surrounds them with a profusion of ferns and other plants.

Nature's endless efforts to colonise the earth with plants cover the most unpromising surfaces with lichens and mosses. Here they provide a nursery for the spiky little koromiko (Hebe salicifolia), one of the first shrubs in the park's plant development cycle.

The New Zealand Dendrobe (Dendrobium cunninghamii) is one of New Zealand's epiphytic, or perching, orchids. They feed on decaying matter and moisture on their host trees.

In a scene typical of Egmont's rain forest, a rata tree on the right winds its roots around an ancient rimu and epiphytes festoon an old giant nearby.

The forests of Egmont National Park provide the visitor with a great range of experiences within a relatively compact area. On Egmont itself, there are distinct zones of vegetation, rising from tall forest with rimu and rata dominant, up through a band of which the kamahi covers two thirds, succeeded by the thin-barked Hall's totara and kaikawaka, or mountain cedar, and then into lower growing plants as the altitude increases. As you emerge from the forest-type vegetation you encounter koromiko, leatherwood and mountain five finger in a dense cover and then into shorter, more hardy trees no taller than a man. Tussock grasses and alpine herbfields then take over and above 1650 m, mosses, lichens and more than 30 different types of flowering plants are found.

Inside the kamahi rain forest of the lower regions, there is sufficient eeriness to conjure up any number of legends about mysterious beings moving on the edge of terror. Moss grows green and thick on twisted limbs and the setting would suit the most grotesque goblin. You can find this kind of green, draped world only a few metres inside the forest near the Stratford Mountain House or the Dawson Falls visitors' centre.

The forest appears to be changing slowly to a kamahi and mahoe type and there has been no replacement of rimu for about 400 years on the slopes of Egmont. Both the rimu and northern rata are gradually disappearing, the latter because of its dependence on the rimu. The rata-rimu association is one of the curiosities of the New Zealand bush and there are excellent examples of it on the Egmont park roads.

The rata starts its life from seed lodging in the forks of rimu trees. The rata sends aerial roots down to the ground and eventually overtops the rimu and robs it of light, ultimately causing its death. The tale that the rata actually strangles the rimu is a myth.

The forest of the park suffers from the usual depredations of goats and opossums. Here again the protection of the forest requires draconian measures against these damaging browsers.

Moss-laden kamahi forms the eerie goblin forest of the park.

A short walk up to Curtis Ridge from the road end above the Mountain House puts visitors among sub-alpine scrub and provides views of the rugged and broken nature of the lava surfaces, cut here and there by streams, with sudden bluffs showing the scale of the eruptions and lava flows. Above alpine tussock, autumn whirls the first snow on to the mountain.

Its distant appearance to the contrary, Mt Egmont is at first hand a broken and rough mountain, with a variety of terrain and a range of features which greatly increase the pleasures of walking the park's 300 km of cut tracks. It is no wonder that the people of Taranaki make such great use of the park. It was they who in fact began the track system and developed it during the late 1800s. Their work laid the foundation for one of the best track networks of any of our national parks. There are two round-the-mountain routes, one at a lower altitude using cut tracks.

On the mountain there is a stream for every day of the year. Every stream has its gully or gorge. Waterfalls abound and Lake Dive is a surprising contrast to the steep slopes of Fanthams Peak.

It is relatively easy to climb to the summit of Egmont in summer and local climbing and mountaineering clubs offer special climbs to the public from time to time. Don't attempt it without guidance from someone who knows the mountain because weather conditions can change quickly. Climbing and skiing attract many thousands of visitors to the park every year.

Mt Egmont is one of the most accessible of national parks and this has helped to give it a dangerous reputation. Many lives have been lost on the mountain and it is essential to remember that a rapid change in the weather can turn a pleasant walk or climb into a fatal venture.

The mountain's dominance on the Taranaki skyline gives the park a singularly well-defined identity. But it is worth remembering that the park protects not only a great visual and recreational area but also the source of an immense network of radiating rivers which carry the mountain's blessing down to the green farmland which surrrounds it.

The tiny *Drapetes dieffenbachii.*

J. Drydon

J. Drydon

The upper tussock and herbfield areas of Mt Egmont sprinkle it with gentle colour in summer. Mountain foxglove *(Ourisia macrophylla)* lays down this carpet. Other plants shown on these pages are part of these varied communities.

Mountain snowberry *(Gaultheria depressa).*

J. Drydon

46

Prominent among Egmont's sub-alpine scrub is the hardy leatherwood *(Senecio elaeagnifolius)*, its name descriptive of its thick leaves. It is the basic plant of this scrub and provides a protective shield for other plants. This photograph shows the wonderful variety of plant life high up on the mountain.

The snow buttercup *(Ranunculus nivicolus)*, one of the splendid family of native mountain buttercups.

J. Drydon

47

Abel Tasman National Park

The first iron anchor which dropped into the sands of Aotearoa fastened to the land both a ship and the first thread of a new civilisation.

The orange sands into which the anchor sank are one of the distinctive features of historic Abel Tasman National Park.

Here occurred the first encounter between Maori and pakeha. It ended in a tragic clash of cultures and of arms.

Off the eastern end of Golden Bay are the Tata Islands and somewhere near them the great Dutch navigator, Abel Tasman, anchored his two ships, the *Heemskirk* and *Zeehaen*, in 1642. He wanted wood and water.

On the night of their arrival, Tasman and his crew saw fires burning in Maori villages on shore and heard strange music drifting across the water. In the morning, several canoes of Maori came out to examine these wonderfully large vessels. The Maori were clearly undeterred by the sight of white faces or the size of the ships and were prepared to offer hostilities.

Attempts at friendship and the offer of gifts by the Europeans were rejected and this fateful meeting ended quickly when a canoe rammed a ship's boat and the Maori killed four sailors in a brief fight. Tasman fought off the attackers, rescued the wounded and put out to sea, pursued by more canoes.

It was a bad start to a new era and it received ugly recognition in Tasman's naming of Murderers Bay, the first European name bestowed on New Zealand. Curiously, Tasman's name is commemorated on this coast only because of an uncharacteristic mistake by the thorough French explorer Dumont D'Urville, who assumed wrongly that Captain Cook had, during his circumnavigation of 1770, so named it.

In fact Cook had given the name of Blind Bay to what we now call Tasman Bay and Tasman's anchorage should have given his name to what is now Golden Bay.

The golden sands and sculpted rocks of the foreshore of Abel Tasman National Park tell a story many millions of years old.

A monument to Tasman's discovery of New Zealand stands near Tarakohe beside the northern road into the park. The best commemoration, though, is the park itself, established in 1942 to mark the third centenary of Tasman's arrival.

The unusual orange beaches, the rocky headlands climbing out of the sea, the islands, inlets, bays and coves of a fretted coast, and the forested hills heaving up inland give the park a blend of land and sea splendours.

Facing out into the lonely waters of western Cook Strait, the park might be on the rim of the world. With the sea on one side and the barrier of the Pikikiruna Range on the other, the park has a sense of remoteness even although it is not set in a wilderness area. This impression is made into a practicality by the fearsome road you take to get into it. Those who know the park would not have it any other way.

When writing his diary of the voyage which brought him to a Nelson summer in 1827, D'Urville recorded the pleasure which he and his crew found off the coast of the park. It is only fair to note that D'Urville was helped by the Maori when he became the second European seafarer to visit the region and that they offered nothing but kindness to the people who founded Nelson when their three ships anchored here in 1841.

A seafaring history of this kind is appropriate to the park and is one of its special historic features. About half its boundary is coastline and it includes the Tata Islands and the other islands of Tonga, Adele (named for D'Urville's wife), Fisherman and Ngaio. The Astrolabe roadstead between Adele Island and the mainland is named for D'Urville's ship. The park extends only an average of 10 km inland and is the smallest of our national parks, with an area of some 22,000 ha.

The park offers good fishing, boating and sailing and it is possible off its coast to experience the same kind of pristine impressions of beckoning beaches and bays under tall hills which the first explorers would have felt.

The landward entry to the park is very different. You must first cross the formidable Takaka Hill, where the road rises from sea level to 791 m in just a few kilometres to cross the Pikikiruna Range. Here you are travelling over rock which is about 425 million years old – about as remote a past as New Zealand can proffer – and the results of the geological process which created the park landscape can be seen in the fantastic rock shapes along the top of the hill. When you step on the sands of the park's beaches you are walking on the last stage of aeons of land building and decay.

Quiet beaches dreaming under native bush offer a secluded place in which to linger.

Abel Tasman National Park's sense of remoteness on the edge of the land comes partly from its uncrowded beaches.

The sedimentary rock of the Pikikiruna Range was formed when New Zealand consisted only of northwest Nelson and Fiordland and was joined to Australia. More than 100 million years ago, molten granite from deep within the earth's crust was forced upwards into this rock, the consequent heat and pressure changing it into marbles and schists.

This great hump of granite forms the main rock on which the park is founded. It and the older rock were carried high above the sea by a stupendous planetary upheaval which, about 20 million years ago, began to thrust up the high peaks of New Zealand along with the Himalayas, the Sierras of North America and part of the South American Andes. The marble which has weathered into freakish shapes on Takaka Hill is a remnant of the older rock type, while the sands of the park's beaches come from weathering of the granite.

The destructive process goes on underground too. The local country contains some extremely fine examples of landforms which develop in marble and limestone through the solvent properties of water. They are called Karst landscapes after a district in Yugoslavia which is famous for its caves, springs and disappearing rivers.

Just outside the park are the deepest cave system and largest springs in New Zealand. The Harwoods Hole-Starlight cave system is 357m deep and the Waikoropupu Springs pour out more than 1,200 million litres of water a day. Water is enlarging the caves by carrying away 253 tonnes, of rock a year and at this rate, Takaka Hill will eventually contain the largest cave system in the southern hemisphere.

On the coast, the sea is working away at the granite and forming caves like those at Anapai beach (the name means good cave) and pillars of granite shorn away from the cliffs.

The Wainui, Awaroa, Torrent Bay and Marahau inlets, which help to make the varied coastline one of the attractions of the park, were gouged out by rivers cutting through softer rock down to levels which were drowned by the seas as the Ice Age came to an end about 14,000 years ago.

The coastal walks at Abel Tasman National Park are not surpassed anywhere in New Zealand. Between Totaranui and Separation Point, which divides Tasman and Golden Bays and where a lighthouse stands, is a walk of about three hours. A well made and maintained track dips down to beaches and up again, hoisting you over headlands, carrying you spider-sidling along steep cliff faces from which you look down into clear water frilled white around the land's toes while bush or scrub sprinkles sunlight on your path. No walk suspends you more dramatically between bush and sea.

You can swim safely from the superb

beaches of Anapai and Mutton Cove on the walk to Separation Point. You can indeed walk the whole coastline from Maharau at the southern end of the park to Separation Point.

Beach fossickers, serious biology students and shell collectors will find the park the most rewarding in the national network. More than 600 of New Zealand's 2000 species of shellfish are found in Cook Strait. Among them are tusk shells, so named because of their resemblance to an elephant's tusk, which come from the sea floor and are seldom washed up on land but which you may find here if you are lucky. Octopuses and squid are found around the park's shores and paua, mussels and other edible shellfish abound.

Away from the sea, the park is rugged and for the most part heavily-bushed, although there is considerable regeneration yet to come on the seaward slopes where early settlers burned the forest. There is much variety in the park vegetation, which includes both North Island subtropical type and South Island rain forest. There is beech forest and natural shrubland dominated by tall manuka and kanuka.

As elsewhere, the park's forests are subject to attack by introduced browsing animals like goats and opossums, the latter being released in

Rocks, sand and clouds are caught in graphic combination.

These rocks represent the final stages of land building and decay which is evident in the park's natural history.

Totaranui has a warm summer welcome for visitors to one of New Zealand's most pleasant camping areas.

1890 by the Nelson Acclimatisation Society for a fur industry – which shows that ignorance is more effective than good intentions. Stoats, ferrets and wild cats affect bird life.

The summit of the Pikikiruna Range forms the western boundary of the park and from here the land drops steeply down in ridges and gullies to the sea. D'Urville noted the steepness of the rivers and streams and the name of Torrent Bay accurately reflects the nature of the land.

The summit plateau is unusual among South Island mountain areas for its relatively flat topography and at the southern or Canaan end, it has one peculiar feature. This is a large basis of sub-alpine tussock and scrub which is biologically out of character at a height of less than 1,000 m.

Plant life here is found nowhere else in the park and would normally be found at much higher altitudes. It has been suggested that this occurs because the basin traps cold air and there is a high water table which reduces oxygen in the soil and inhibits the growth of big trees. The tussockland is similar to the upper parts of the central volcanic plateau of the North Island.

The road to Canaan is off the Motueka-Takaka road and is worth at least a brief visit because it passes through a splendid Karst landscape and provides outstanding views of Nelson and Tasman Bay. Canaan is the start or finish point for a number of walking tracks through the higher parts of the park, including a walk of nine or ten hours between Canaan and Totaranui, mostly through bush.

The warm-temperate rain forest has a rich plant life under the main canopy, with many perchers and climbers, ferns, shrubs and trees.

Forest and sea are the main visual elements of the park. This view of the coastline from the Lookout Rock track shows the prolific rain forest.

J. Du

There are many shorter walks and one which shows the variety of the park is from the Totaranui-Awaroa road through bush to the sea and along the Goat Bay beach to Totaranui. The beauty of the bush is well shown by the emergence of the track here and there into clearings made in the old timber milling days. Part of the track follows the old bush tramway which took logs down to the sawmill near Waiharakeke Beach. A rock cutting for the tramway is still visible.

Another easy walk is from the Totaranui road to Lookout Rock. This passes through beautiful rain forest to a rock pinnacle with tremendous views of Wainui Inlet, Golden Bay, Cape Farewell and Farewell Spit. Points of interest are marked along the track and one thing to look out for is honey dew produced by a mealybug which lives on the bark of beech trees. The black mould characteristic of beech grows on the honeydew, to which wasps will lead your eye.

Living in the highest reaches of the park is the large land snail, whose local variety of *Powelliphanta* has a shell up to 75 mm in diameter and bandings ranging from dark browns to gold and cream. The shell is highly polished. The snails are rare and can live only among the cool and moist forest on the mountain ridges.

Walking is a rewarding activity in the park and visitors who take the time to explore away from the beaches will gain much from their experience of the complementary attractions of bush and seacoast.

The sea's nibbling edge has its effects on the granite floor of the park.

This view of Anapai Bay from the Headland track sums up the contrast between bush and sea.

Totaranui is the site of the park's headquarters and of the only camping ground, which seems to have more space for each visitor than probably any other in the southern hemisphere. For sensible park management reasons, the ground is restricted to a maximum of 800 people and bookings are advisable between December 15 and January 15.

Totaranui still has signs of past colonial splendour. One of Nelson's best known settlers, William Gibbs, established an estate here which marked the transition of the district from Maori occupation to European settlement.

The Maori had first been attracted from the North Island to the coastline of the park, with its shelter and seafood, during the 13th Century. They hunted moa here and artifacts of the moa hunter period have been found at Anapai, Awaroa and Adele Island.

There is a major gap in modern knowledge about the Maori history and it can be blamed on Te Rauparaha and his muskets. There had been the usual inter-tribal fighting since the Maori first came to Nelson, but this was minor compared with the 1828 raids by the feared Te Rauparaha. He and his warriors brought muskets which made the killing of men armed with stone and wood a long-distance sporting affair.

The killing of leaders and learned men of the local tribes destroyed traditional knowledge in the region. Subsequently, the spread of firearms and disease by civilising influences from Europe brought to ruin a society which had lasted for 500 years.

The coastline attracted settlers from the 1850s on and the strait was busy with local shipping. Tonga Island provided granite blocks for the Wellington Post Office and Public Trust Office but farming and timber milling were the main sources of livelihood.

William Gibbs was the big figure of those days. He was ambitious, as you can see from the wide avenue of great plane trees and macrocarpas which runs from the beach across the Totaranui flat to the old homestead. Along this avenue, which one of Gibb's daughters helped to plant, a small carriage drawn by a cream pony used to carry visitors from a landing jetty up to the house and gardens. Here were ornamental fruit trees, lawns, flower beds, a fountain and a goldfish pond about the gabled, two-storied house.

This dedicated farmer, Member of Parliament, Member of the Nelson Provincial Council, Justice of the Peace and father of eight children, was famous for his hospitality and Totaranui was regarded as the showpiece of the coast. Part of its history is visible in the old homestead which Gibb's eldest son built and which is now used to accommodate school parties. The original home was burned down in the 1920s.

Awaroa was another well established settlement in the 1850s and many large homes were built here. Torrent Bay also attracted settlement and looking at it today, you assume that one of the reasons was the loveliness of the place. Torrent Bay's headlands, reefs and islands are among the best physical assets of the park and several inland walks allow a closer acquaintance with the area.

One of the Gibbs family's old homesteads at Totaranui is now used for school party accommodation. Native forest is regenerating on the hill above where the Gibbs once farmed.

This footprint marker is both a guide and a reminder that footprints should be the only signs left by man in our national parks.

Learning about the immense variety of life, children explore miniature worlds among the rocks.

Nelson Lakes National Park

Of all the legacies left by the work of glaciers on the New Zealand landscape, none is more beautiful than the stretching waters around which Nelson Lakes National Park has been created.

Lakes Rotoiti and Rotoroa are a couplet of nature's rhyming. They lie in two great troughs scooped out by the glaciers of the Ice Age and each has its guarding amphitheatre of mountains springing steeply up from the water's edge. With their almost identical settings, these lakes are Castor and Pollux of New Zealand's scenic constellations, with each the other's peer. No more subtle comparison of features lies among New Zealand's mountains.

Of course people who get in among the bush, high peaks, deep valleys, wide river flats and steep streams of Nelson Lakes National Park know that while the lakes have been the park's genesis, they are also a starting point for many challenges and recreational diversions for trampers, climbers, fishermen, hunters and skiers. It is one of New Zealand's most rewarding areas for recreational diversity which is within the capacity of a wide band of ages and degrees of physical fitness. That is why it has been called a middle-aged mountaineer's mecca, but it is no less grand for that.

The park is formed of the entire catchment areas of the two lakes, and mountain uplift has placed these catchments high above sea level. The uplift is part of the process which gave rise to the Southern Alps and the same alpine fault which created them has given the park some distinctive natural features. The lakes lie more or less on the doorstep of the park and behind them to the south the land rises back into the ranges and valleys which make up the catchments.

Beech trees frame this summer view of Lake Rotoiti from the Kerr Bay foreshore. The motor camp here is a popular base in summer for exploring the mountains, valleys and rivers of the park. Lake Rotoiti is an important water recreation centre for the northern part of the South Island.

The New Zealand alpine fault, that great score across time and country, has created the high land of the park and placed Lake Rotoiti 164m above Lake Rotoroa. The fault, described more fully in the chapter on Westland National Park, has here raised the land to the southeast higher than the land to the northwest. The fault line passes by the outlet of Lake Rotoiti and the head of Lake Rotoroa on its long march to Fiordland. Like pendants turned in opposite directions on a thread, Rotoiti lies within the higher land on one side of the fault while Rotoroa lies along the lower land on the other side. The fault makes a natural boundary to the park's ranges but if it were the park boundary, Rotoroa would fall outside it. Movement along the fault has been going on for millions of years and it continues today. Nelson Lakes National Park offers one of the best opportunities to see the fault, which is revealed in a trench-like formation crossing the peninsula which juts into Lake Rotoiti at St Arnaud township.

The ranges of the park, together with the main rivers, lie in a north-south direction and their northern ends are sharply truncated where earth movement along the fault has thrust the land up to form the mountains. The uplift has made the ranges which flank Rotoiti higher than those rising from the sides of Rotoroa. The Muntz and Braeburn Ranges alongside Rotoroa are no higher than 1200-1400 m, but the main ranges in the remainder of the park rise commonly over 1600 m with many peaks more than 2000 m high. However the views up both lakes from their outlets have striking similarities in their glacial origins and the high mountains from which their respective rivers emerge to feed them.

Both lakes have the steep sides characteristic of the vast abrasive power of the Ice Age glaciers but the ice carved a deeper lake in Rotoroa. Its maximum depth is 145 m compared with 82 m in Rotoiti and it is 14.4 km long and 445 m above sea level. Rotoiti is 8 km long and 609 m above sea level. Three main rivers flow south to north to feed the lakes, the Travers running into Rotoiti and the Sabine and D'Urville into Rotoroa. They flow virtually parallel with one another between the ranges – from east to west the St Arnaud, Travers, Mahanga and Ella – so that the park is very much a finger-like arrangement of mountains and valleys. The highest peak is Mt Franklin, its 2339 m placing it just 1 m above Mt Travers. These two mountains, together with Mt Mackay, Mt Cupola and Kehu Peak, form the quintet which plays the loftiest notes in most views from either lake.

Lake Rotoiti is the source of the Buller River, the principal river of the northern part of the South Island, which is joined by the Gowan River out of Lake Rotoroa. Lake Rotoiti is impounded by a big heap of rock and gravel which has been left as a memento of the final advance and retreat

Lake Rotoiti from the eastern shore. Snow paints the Travers Range and, behind it, the St Arnaud Range. Steep mountain sides are typical of glacier-formed lake beds.

of the Ice Age glaciers which formed the lake beds. Known as a terminal moraine (moraine is the deposited rock and rubble scoured off the country by glacier ice during its journey), it makes a prominent ridge at St Arnaud township. The road from the main highway down to the lake foreshore passes up and over this moraine, which will give you a manifest demonstration of a glacier's past energy. Large blocks of rock scattered around the moraine are part of the glacier's deposits. The terminal moraine at Lake Rotoroa has been largely destroyed by the Gowan River but signs of it remain about 1 km down the river from the lake outlet.

Although Nelson Lakes National Park is readily accessible, with a main highway at its doorstep, its essential character is much the same as when Europeans first discovered it, although introduced animals and previous farming have had their effects on vegetation. The notable example is the north face of Mt Robert, which is a testament to foolish grazing practice. But still the bush for the most part marches in crowding hosts from water's edge and valley floor to snowline and the park terrain enfolds you away from civilisation. Its 57,000 ha are few enough to allow much more than a nodding aquaintance with it but intimacy will only improve appreciation.

The first Europeans to see Lake Rotoiti were John Cotterell, a 23-year-old surveyor and explorer, and Richard Painter, who with their Maori guide Kehu arrived there on January 18, 1843. All three names are commemorated among the peaks of the St Arnaud Range. It is worth reflecting on this Maori Kehu. Much deserved praise has been heaped on the great European explorers of New Zealand. Yet the Maori were perhaps as great and a long time before them.

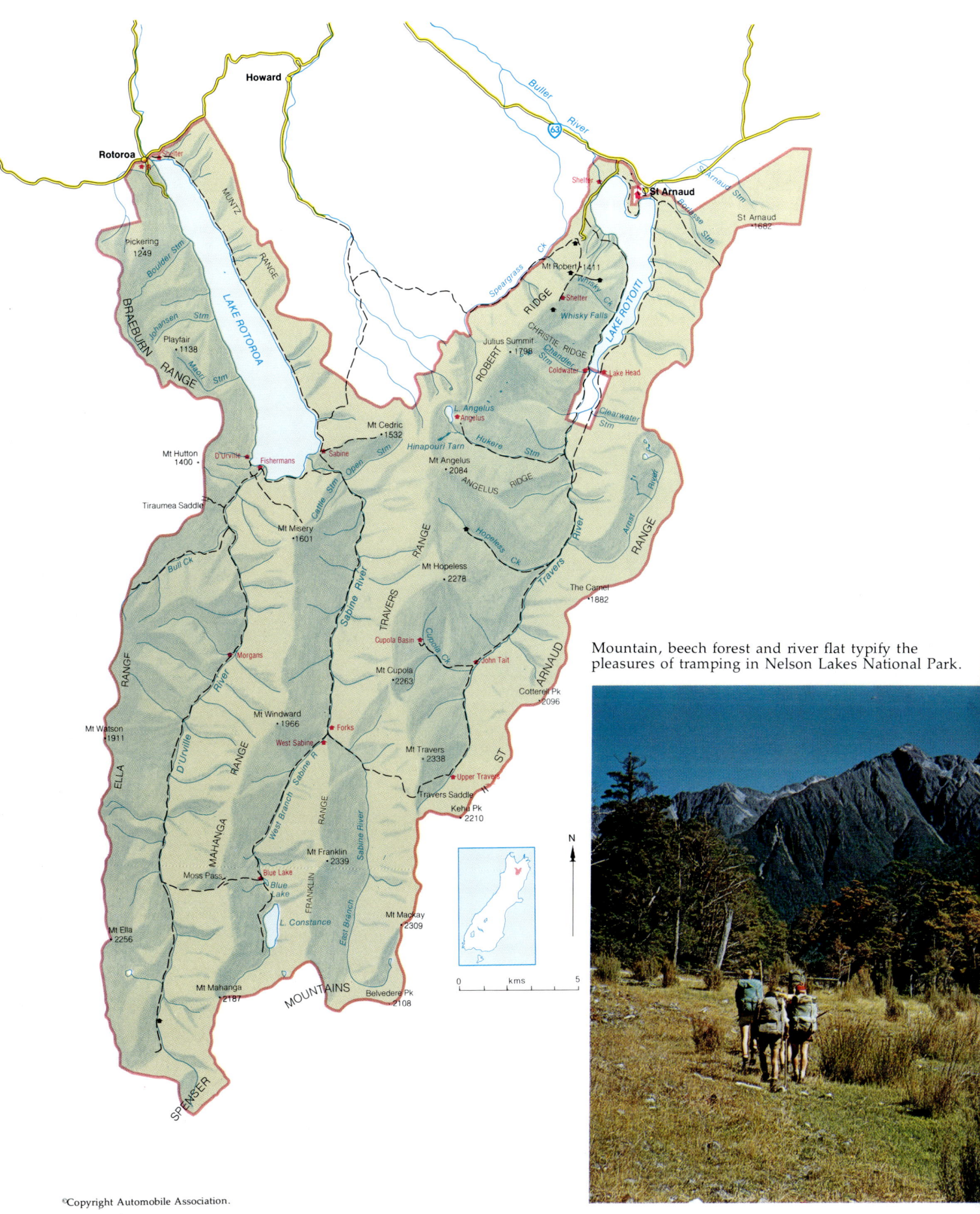

Mountain, beech forest and river flat typify the pleasures of tramping in Nelson Lakes National Park.

Map Labels

Howard

Buller River

63

Rotoroa

Shelter

Pickering 1249

Boulder Stm

BRAEBURN RANGE

Johansen Stm

Playfair 1138

Maui Stm

MUNTZ RANGE

LAKE ROTOROA

Mt Hutton 1400

D'Urville

Fishermans

Tiraumea Saddle

Cattle Stm

Sabine

Open

Mt Cedric 1532

Sabine Stm

Hinapouri Tarn

L. Angelus

Angelus

Hukere Stm

Mt Angelus 2084

ANGELUS RIDGE

Bull Ck

Mt Misery 1601

TRAVERS RANGE

Mt Hopeless 2278

Hopeless Ck

Travers River

Shelter

St Arnaud

St Arnaud Stm

Boulder Stm

St Arnaud 1682

Speargrass Ck

Mt Robert 1411

Whisky Ck

Shelter

Whisky Falls

CHRISTIE RIDGE

ROBERT RIDGE

Julius Summit 1798

Chandler Stm

Coldwater

Lake Head

LAKE ROTOITI

Clearwater Stm

Arnst River

ST ARNAUD RANGE

The Camel 1882

Morgans

D'Urville River

ELLA RANGE

Mt Watson 1911

MAHANGA RANGE

Cupola Basin

Cupola Ck

Mt Cupola 2263

Mt Windward 1966

Forks

West Sabine

West Branch Sabine R

Sabine River

John Tait

Cotterell Pk 2096

Mt Travers 2338

Upper Travers

Travers Saddle

Kehu Pk 2210

Moss Pass

Blue Lake

Blue Lake

FRANKLIN RANGE

Mt Franklin 2339

L. Constance

East Branch Sabine River

Mt Mackay 2309

Mt Ella 2256

Mt Mahanga 2187

SPENSER MOUNTAINS

Belvedere Pk 2108

N

0   kms   5

There was a certain amount of sniffing at claims by Maori like Kehu to know areas which the Europeans had yet to discover. Kehu took Cotterell to Rotoiti. In 1840 he patiently guided William Fox and the incomparable Thomas Brunner to their discovery of Lake Rotoroa, after Charles Heaphy had earlier failed to find it – without Kehu. It was the faithful Kehu who led Brunner on his immortal, but painful and laborious, journey from Nelson to Paringa, on the West Coast, and back. It took 560 days and ranks as New Zealand's greatest single journey of exploration, although chroniclers forget that Kehu and his wife, together with another Maori couple, suffered all of the hardships which broke Brunner's health. To have such a guide was surely fortunate.

Having seen Lake Rotoroa, Fox, later to become four times Prime Minister of New Zealand, wrote that it would make a good watering place for invalids from India. Lucklily it has been left mostly to the bush and the birds. Fox's painting of the lake, in the Alexander Turnbull Library, reflects his captivation.

You can still get a fine sense of discovery from coming upon either of these beautiful lakes, ruffling themselves among the silent mountains. But for tracks, huts and the odd river swingbridge, development is restricted to the outskirts of the park – St Arnaud village and the Mt Robert skifield at Rotoiti, a motorcamp and minimal facilities at Rotoroa. There is at Rotoiti a piquant contrast between summer – yachts, speedboats, water-skiing, swimming, sunbathing on the beaches – and winter, when snow comes close to the lake and just above it the skis hiss on Mt Robert. Rotoroa offers a further contrast – it is a quieter place than Rotoiti because its development is low-key. Water skiing is not permitted there. Both lakes give the park an aquatic recreational role which no other New Zealand national park has in quite the same way.

Summer opens up the park to many kinds of recreation. Walking, tramping and climbing as well as water-related sports give visitors much freedom to make of the park what they will. Trampers find their own special paradise here. Tracks extend through all of the park's main features and experienced trampers and climbers can make their own paths beyond what is provided. Bush, high grasslands, small lakes and tarns filling old glacier hollows, rocky rivers and valleys opening out into grassy river flats under a blue summer sky are among the pleasures of exploring this park. But you'll need good boots.

The Lake Rotoiti shore offers visitors a warmer welcome than the heights of the St Arnaud Range, its steep face coloured by plants able to survive extremes of temperature among a bed of rock and shingle. The St Arnaud nature walk from Kerr Bay climbs up to these tops.

G. Cobb

Travers River provides an angler with an opportunity to take a trout. The main river flowing into Lake Rotoiti, its valley is one of the most popular tramping routes in the park. Behind is Mt Travers (2338 m), second highest peak in the park.

J. Duncan

The beautiful beech forest on the eastern track around Lake Rotoiti.

Lake Rotoroa lies calmly amid the bare mountains of high summer. The view is from the Porika track.

A tranquil exploration of a corner of Lake Rotoroa provides summer joy for these youngsters.

As in so many of the national parks in this rampant land, there is a wide range of vegetation at Nelson Lakes because of altitude differences, even though this park starts well above sea level. Changes in vegetation at various levels are demonstrated by the lookout track up the St Arnaud Range from Kerr Bay at Lake Rotoiti. This takes you up to an altitude of 1372 m but with time and energy you can continue another few hundred metres to the divide. Your reward will be superb views of both sides of the range and the other mountains. The track passes through beech, rata and kamahi and emerges from the bush into carpet grass and tussock slopes.

Above the bushline you can examine at first hand the nature of the rock which has made the St Arnaud Range so susceptible to erosion, including rockslides which plunge far down into the beech forest to leave vivid scars. Like the Travers Range, the St Arnaud mountains are formed of sand and mud laid down on an ancient sea floor and subsequently hardened by burial several kilometres below later sediments. Their instability under weathering has softened the shapes of the mountain peaks and levelled off the divide. Above the bushline, the range has in summer a peculiarly naked look, made more startling by the band of mauve carpet spread over the rock by plants able to survive these inhospitable conditions.

A shorter walk up Black Hill, by Rotoiti Lodge, is an easier way of introducing yourself to the park's botany. When you reach the top, 127 m above Lake Rotoiti, remind yourself that you are standing on what lay deep under the sea in some primordial time. This is volcanic lava which originally welled up on the ocean floor and was lifted up with the surrounding country by faulting. The two-hour nature walk over the Lake Rotoiti peninsula, part of the moraine left by the retreating glacier, takes you on a track along which many plants are labelled. A walk from the Mt Robert Road to the glacier-carved basins of Robert Ridge, part of the Travers Range, will take you into an interesting area of carpet grass, tussock and, in summer, native flowering plants.

Beech – silver, red, black, mountain – is spread widely around the park and there are stands of kahikatea, rimu and Hall's totara. Kowhai will in a good season sprinkle the edges of Lake Rotoroa with gold, and southern rata will break out a mass of red along Lake Rotoiti. More than 120 mosses, orchids which appear on the forest floor in the spring and varicoloured vegetable sheep growing above the snowline indicate the range of plant life which grows in the park. Native mistletoe used to abound but it has been wiped out by that evil bush bandit, the opossum.

B. Postill

Tussock and sprawling scree slopes at the head of the Travers Valley. The upper Travers hut is by the small beginning of the river.

A snowy woollyhead (*Craspedia incana*) sends up a defiant stalk and flower from its inhospitable rocky bed.

T. Pitman

Clinging precariously where no plant might be expected to grow is a tufted Haastia *(Haastia sinclarii)*.

The giant vegetable sheep *(Haastii pulvinaris)*, one of New Zealand's most remarkable plants, grows among the harsh surroundings of the park scree. These daisy plants have adapted to temperatures ranging from fierce summer heat to acute frosts by developing a form which reduces water loss to a minimum. The plant's surface is composed of the leafy tips of hundreds of densely-packed branches.

T. Pitman

T. Pitman

As well as the shorter walks described at Lake Rotoiti, Lake Rotoroa has several easy tracks which wind through the beautiful beech forest. The Porika track presents a stiff climb to a look-out, but there is from here a fine view of lake and mountains.

A round trip to the head of Lake Rotoiti and back is something which every visitor should walk. It is not difficult and it will allow you to appreciate more closely the scale of the upper reaches of the park. It is just right for a day's outing and there are lovely little bays for picnics and swimming close to the track along the eastern side of the lake. Look out for the only stand of rimu known to grow in the Lake Rotoiti watershed. You can return by the same route or cross the Travers River, if this is low, at the head of the lake and use the track on the western side.

A track runs along the eastern side of Lake Rotoroa between the picnic ground at the outlet end and the head of the lake. It is rougher walking than the eastern track at Lake Rotoiti and walking it one way takes about six hours, so that it is not a realistic target for a day's outing. You can, though, use the Sabine hut at the lake head for overnight accommodation.

The system of huts and tracks throughout the park reflects the high regard in which trampers hold the area. There are 15 Park Board huts with bunks and limited cooking facilities and most parts of the park are within easy walking distance of them.

Walking tracks follow the three main rivers – D'Urville, Sabine and Travers – and others reach up into the valley of tributary streams. The two biggest minor lakes, Constance and Angelus, both carved out by old glaciers, are served by tracks and huts. The track to the former passes beautiful Blue Lake, one of the many tarns, or small mountain lakes, which lie in ice-eroded hollows on the ranges. Round trips using the main valley tracks can be made. Moss Pass over the Mahanga Range connects the upper D'Urville River valley with the west branch of the upper Sabine River. Travers Saddle over the Travers Range links the east branch of the Sabine with the Travers River.

Mountaineering in the park does not offer the high challenges of the Southern Alps but it provides excellent opportunities for learning and for those of an age which is beyond greater challenges. This is a park for mountaineers of many ages and of different levels of experience.

There are many species of birds in the park despite the ravages of stoats, ferrets, wild cats and introduced animals. Many native birds, the native quail, brown duck, saddleback, kokako, kaka, weka, parakeet, yellowhead and bush wren are now rare or have disappeared entirely.The weka and kiwi populations have been much reduced. But you'll still hear and see tomtits, riflemen, bellbirds, tui, grey warbler, fantails and yellow-breasted tits and have a chance to shake hands with the cheeky, knock-kneed robin, a most inquiring and engaging bird. If you have a good ear you'll distinguish many more native birds and might be lucky enough to see a white faced heron, blue duck, New Zealand falcon, spur-winged plover, kea, rock wren and brown creeper.

There is good fishing in the park, with brown trout predominant and the rainbow available in Lake Rotoroa and the Sabine River. Hunting is a popular sport but there is no doubt that the quality of the park would be best protected – and improved – by the complete extermination of red deer and chamois. This aim must override the interest of hunters in keeping a population of these animals for sport. The short and long tailed bat, the only native land mammals of New Zealand, are both found in the park.

Nelson Lakes National Park has, understandably, a special place in the hearts of the people of Nelson and Marlborough. Rotoiti Lodge is an expression of their attitude. Inspired by Mr N. B. Oxnam, a former police sergeant and Park Board member, it was built, with voluntary effort and donated materials, by the people of the two provinces. It has given hundreds of children a chance to get in touch with nature in a park where mountain, lake and bush stand together in a compact which is not duplicated elsewhere in New Zealand.

Beech trees and moss help to sustain each other in the West Sabine Valley. The park's beech forest is haven to many species of native birds.

B. Postill

G. Moon

The tui is New Zealand's most famous flighted bird, with its distinctive little throat tuft, lacy white collar and glossy, blue-green feathers. A nectar feeder, it is common around the valley floors and lower slopes of the park.

The Southern Rata (*Metrosideros umbellata*) in full flower.

The commemorative plaque at Rotoiti Lodge, with kea rampant.

B. Postill

Arthur's Pass National Park

The creation of a national park around a high pass through the Southern Alps reflects in part the early European settlers' pre-occupation with finding a route over the mountains between Canterbury and Westland. Land hunger was the initial impetus and then the discovery of Westland gold made success imperative.

With urgency appeased by the finding of Arthur's Pass and the driving of a road through it, there was time and opportunity for people to appreciate the magnificence of the mountains, forests, rivers and lakes of the surrounding country. The road through the pass led almost inevitably to the idea of a national park and with the discoverer of the pass, Arthur Dudley Dobson, alive to promote it, the idea became a reality in 1929. Dobson, then Sir Arthur, became a member of the first board.

Arthur's Pass National Park is unusual in having sprung directly from a highway but it was a natural development. The pass takes you through the Southern Alps in dramatic fashion – it is the highest of the three passes which lift main highways over the most rugged mountain terrain of the South Island and it allows the least adventurous people to experience and admire New Zealand's alpine grandeur.

Although today's highway is modern and fast to travel on, it still provides some of New Zealand's most spectacular motoring. The zigzag which the highway takes in the Otira Gorge gives a breathtaking ride in a modern car – imagine having to plunge down it on a swaying, jolting coach, with imperfect brakes and perhaps a drunken driver, in rain and wind and mist and snow, with the river roaring just below. Rivers and streams are the permanent accompaniment to driving through the pass, with the Otira River flowing west and the Bealey River flowing east from the main divide at the summit of the pass.

From a ribbon of road connecting Canterbury and Westland across the Southern Alps of New Zealand has developed a national park to preserve the magnificence of the surrounding country.

These rivers caused great difficulty to the earliest users of the pass. Because of its rough nature, the Maori did not use Arthur's Pass regularly on their journeys across the Southern Alps to get greenstone in the Arahura and Taramakau Valleys. They preferred the Hurunui Saddle, by the source of the Hurunui River at the north-east corner of the park. This was renamed Harpers Pass after Leonard Harper, who crossed it in November, 1857, with a companion under the guidance of four Maori from Kaiapohia (Kaiapoi). Although the Maori had long used this pass, Harper was not even the first European to cross it. He had been preceeded in September by Edward Dobson, Engineer to the Canterbury Provincial Government, although Dobson had not travelled far over the pass, while Harper went on to the West Coast. As we shall see, the Dobson family played a unique role in the story of Arthurs Pass. But before they did, Samuel Butler, novelist ('Erewhon'), satirist, essayist and scholar, almost gave his name to Arthur's Pass. One of the searchers for sheep grazing land to the west of the mountains, Butler, seeking the fortune which would allow him to devote the remainder of his life to writing, explored many of the great upper river valleys of Canterbury. In 1860 he travelled up the Bealey River and saw the low saddle of the pass, but was reluctant to leave his horse to clamber up to it.

As in other parts of New Zealand, it was the Maori who showed the pakeha the way to exploration. They gave white men advice on bushcraft, routes through the mountains, how to catch birds and eels and how several people could cross rivers safely by linking arms and clutching a long pole – an unsurpassed method still used today. They also fed and cared for many white travellers who would otherwise have starved.

In July, 1863, a gold rush from Canterbury to Westland began. The destination was Greenstone in the lower Taramakau Valley, with gold replacing greenstone as the prize for which men had to journey over the Southern Alps. Immediately the Harpers Pass route became a trampled highway. By 1865 the gold workings were in full swing and the rough track across the mountains was crowded with endless trains of diggers, pack horses, pedlars, scoundrels and cattle being driven over to feed the hungry miners – in 1865-66, more than 4400 cattle went over the pass and the mud was abominable.

Better things were on the way though and the Dobsons brought them. Edward Dobson, the Canterbury Provincial Engineer, had three sons, Arthur Dudley, who was a surveyor for the Canterbury Provincial Government, and George and Edward. In February, 1864, Arthur and Edward, respectively aged only 23 and 18, set out to find a better route than Harpers Pass for the supplies Arthur needed on his surveying trips. They rode up the Waimakariri and Mingha Rivers and then

came to the swampy valley which had once been the bed of a glacier – the Bealey River valley. They walked over a glacial moraine at the end of the valley with their barometer showing 3000ft. They had crossed the pass, the first white men to do so.

Over the pass they found 'a very precipitous descent into a long, narrow gorge,' that of the Otira River. The two brothers travelled down the gorge, an undertaking full of obstacles, and Arthur foresaw the amount of rock which would have to be cut for a road. Such a project did not seem feasible. But in 1865, with the gold rush at its peak, the Provincial Government asked George Dobson, Arthur's brother, to see whether the Bealey-Otira Rivers route was suitable for a road. In a report to the Government, George dismissed 'Arthur's Pass' as a possibility and the name gradually became permanent. The search for an alternative route continued but there was none and Edward Dobson senior decided to put a road through the pass named after his son.

A horse track went through in 1865 and work began straight after on a metalled road which was completed in the following year. That was a remarkable engineering feat without machinery to bite, stamp and gouge the country into submission. The pace was restricted to the slice of a shovel, the capacity of a wheelbarrow, the power of a pick, the swing of an axe. The cost of the road between Christchurch and Hokitika was £145,000, a considerable price in those days. Arthur Dobson was involved in the building of the road on the Westland side of the main divide.

Arthurs Pass National Park

The Dobson Memorial at the summit of the pass.

Permanent snow on Mt Rolleston (2270 m) feeds the Bealey River, one of the two rivers whose valleys provided the way through the Southern Alps.

There are several other main divide passes in the park, but Arthur's Pass is the lowest at 920 m. Harpers Pass is 960 m but it provides a longer route between Christchurch and the West Coast and became a minor track with the opening of the Arthur's Pass road. Today it is a trampers' preserve. In 1866 a telegraph line was put through the pass and in that year the new road's importance was demonstrated by the driving of 40,000 sheep and 25,000 cattle through to the miners in Westland. There was farming in the pass and other parts of the park and much of the original vegetation was destroyed to make way for it, the results being seen today in scrub and weed invasion.

Arthur's Pass had one of New Zealand's longest-lived coaching services, which began in 1866 to service the Westland gold fields. The mining boom was over by 1870 but the coach continued until the Otira rail tunnel was opened in 1923, its run becoming progressively shorter as the railway was extended towards the pass from each side of the Southern Alps. By 1876 there was a railway from Greymouth to Brunner and four years later a line had reached Springfield from Christchurch.

The Otira Tunnel which carries the railway under the pass was started in 1908 by a private company which was unable to cope with construction and money problems and handed the project over to the Government in 1912. The same problems had caused the Government to take over the extension of the railways, which reached Otira from the west in 1900 but did not arrive at Arthur's Pass from the east until 1915. The tunnel was driven through in 1918 and opened in 1923 after lining, tracklaying and the running of electric overhead wires – electric traction was chosen to avoid tunnel ventilation problems with steam engines.

Building the 9.45 km tunnel was a deservedly famous engineering feat. It became on completion the seventh longest tunnel in the world and drew international popular attention to the magnitude of the Southern Alps. Its engineering accuracy was high indeed – the differences between calculation and final result were 91 cm for length, less than 3 cm for level and less than 2 cm for alignment. It was a noble accomplishment by New Zealand engineers and it remains a tunnel of international ranking.

While men strove with road and rail links across the pass, a quieter campaign was being conducted to preserve the scenery which crowds so mightily around the pass. At the instigation initially of Dr Leonard Cockayne, a naturalist who first visited the park area in 1898 and later had a cottage at Kellys Creek in the Otira valley, the Government reserved in 1901 almost 7000 ha in the Otira valley and 20,000 ha in the Waimakariri Valley for a future national park. In the 1920s the discoverer of the pass, Sir Arthur

Dobson, and Canterbury organisations, among them the Canterbury Mountaineering Club, stepped up the campaign and the park was formed in 1929. The appointment of Sir Arthur to the first Park Board rounded off a family connection with the pass and the park which has a singular place in our history. The park is the fourth largest in the network, with almost 100,000 ha, so that it is much more than a pass.

As with other national parks in the southern part of the South Island, Arthur's Pass National Park owes its underlying character to the forces which thrust up the Southern Alps and created a wall of mountains which were then eroded into jagged peaks, deep valleys, landslides and screes and the courses of rivers, streams and waterfalls. This broken, rugged and beautiful landscape extends as far as about 15 km to the west of the main highway and some 30 km to the east.

Although this park does not have the high peaks of the Southern Alps further to the south, it towers over the plains to east and west, with 16 named mountains more than 2000 m high. The main divide of the Southern Alps lies more or less through the middle of the park, topped by Mt Murchison at 2400 m. The park's location therefore gives it the distinction of displaying on its mountain sides two dissimilar kinds of vegetation – the rain forest of Westland and the beech forest of Canterbury. Another distinguishing feature is the refreshingly original names of two of the high mountains, Bloody Limit and Damfool. One cannot begin to guess at the kind of experiences someone was going through when these names were given.

Arthurs Pass National Park

A brilliant display of southern rata (*Metrosideros umbellata*) blossoms above the tortuous Otira zigzag on the western side of the main divide of the Southern Alps. Although it grows thickly here, the rata is absent on the other side of the divide.

The great Alpine Fault of New Zealand has influenced this park as it has other parks and the mountains, to the east of the fault line, are still rising. Don't worry, you won't notice the movement, although an earthquake may occur to remind you of the tremendous pressures stored up in the earth's slowly moving crust. When pressure overcomes friction and the rocks slide against one another earthquakes occur like the one of 1929, the so-called Murchison earthquake. Here in the park it had one conspicuously evident result – the collapse of an enormous part of Falling Mountain, which sent hundreds of thousands of tonnes of rock cascading 5 km down the Otehake Valley area. The earthquake also caused considerable damage in the Hawdon and Poulter Valleys. An older landslide formed Lake Minchin, on a tributary of the Poulter River, and the main highway crosses another huge pile of fallen rock at its high point just above the Otira zigzag.

Large screes – sloping beds of loose rock brought down from the mountains by avalanche and other erosion – are significant features of the park landscape. There are prominent examples east of the Otira zigzag, on the other side of the highway in the upper Otira valley and at the top of the Bealey River. The name of Avalanche Peak is descriptive of the crumbling nature of the rock in the park and so are the wide gravel beds through which the larger rivers go their rambling way. The cause is the effect of temperature extremes on the soft rock, freezing and cracking it in winter, washing it down in summer with rain and meltwater from the winter snow. These shingle river beds are very deep, filling up the floors of valleys which were milled by glaciers during the Ice Age, when the whole park area was filled with ice covering all but the highest peaks. Such rivers, characteristic of the South Island, are found in very few other places in the world. Millions of years of erosion since the Southern Alps were built has formed them. The glaciers contributed much to this process by grinding material from the mountains and carrying it down to the Canterbury Plains – the Waimakariri Glacier once reached Springfield, about 55 km east of the main divide.

The braided river bed of the Waimakariri gleams between beech forest and mountains.

The highest peak in the park, Mt Murchison (2400 m), stands above White River, a tributary of the Waimakariri River. The blue-grey rock is typical of the park riverbeds in the high reaches of the valleys and illustrates the rough travelling which faced the early explorers.

Weather is the elemental cause of this scouring and in the park the main divide of the Southern Alps has a fundamental effect. Westerly winds are usually funnelling through the park's valleys and vaulting over the peaks, bringing a lot of rain, but often in very heavy falls so that the park also enjoys long periods of fine weather. It is possible to approach the main divide from the east in fine weather and to cross the summit of the pass into wind and rain on the west. The effect of the western mountain slope on the prevailing winds is shown by an average annual rainfall of 5000mm at Otira, 4000mm at Arthur's Pass village and – only 8 km further east – 1500 mm at Bealey. Snow is heavy in winter but there are also consecutive days of bright blue skies arching over a bright white landscape.

Differences in rainfall on each side of the main divide contribute materially to the pattern of park vegetation. On the west, the heavy and frequent rainfall typical of Westland has fed a dense and tall podocarp forest of matai, kahikatea, miro and totara. There is rimu on the higher slopes and associated plants are lowland ribbonwood, kamahi, fuchsia, marble-leaf (putaputaweta), quintinia and a variety of shrubs, vines and climbers. The forests of Westland are well provided with fuchsia, which are indigenous only to New Zealand, Mexico and South America. Our species are a herb, a shrub, a climber and a tree. There are many more ferns and mosses here than on the eastern side of the divide. Mountain, or Hall's, totara is a dominant tree on the upper western slopes, with neinei, that strange and luxuriant tree likened to the pineapple, cedar and pink pine sprinkled about. A summer glory is the flowering of the southern rata on the western mountain sides in a good season – about one in every three years. This tree out-blossoms the northern rata and the North Island's pohutukawa and the New Zealand forest has no more glorious spectacle than when it lays its crimson blanket over the forest canopy. The tree does not grow in the park to the east of the divide – a remarkable example of plant discrimination in view of the banked masses of rata on the western side. Unfortunately, the rata rates highly as food for the introduced opossums, whose inclinations are revealed by dead tops scattered through the forest canopy. The park's eastern forests are mostly mountain beech, with some good stands of red and silver beech, especially in the Poulter valley.

Arthurs Pass National Park

A view down the Poulter Valley from Worsley Pass shows how a meandering river has kept the thick beech forest at bay. The valley floor is built up from centuries of erosion which has carried debris down from the mountains to form deep shingle beds. The Poulter Valley is one of the most popular long tramping routes in the park.

Tramping under the steep face of Carrington Peak (2026 m). Throughout the park, raw rock and varied vegetation provide a dramatic contrast.

Mt Rolleston (2270 m) in mid-winter.

Devils Punchbowl Falls (150 m) throw a silver stream between the rich green of the beech forest.

TARAMAKAU RIVER
Locke Stm

KELLY RANGE
Aickens

Kellys Hill
Carroll
1396
Kelly Shelter
Pfeifer Ck
L. Kaurapataka
Mt Koeti
1783
DIVIDE

Mt Pfeifer
1703
Hot Spring
MAIN
CUP RA
Mt Row
1679

OTIRA
Goat Hill
1649
Sulphur Spring
Mt Tarapuhi
1609
Mt McRae
1750
Thompson
1722
L. Minchin
Mt Morrison
1722

Mt Barron
1725
Otira Gorge
Mt Russel
1850
OTEHAKE WILDERNESS AREA
Worsley
POULTER RANGE

BARRON RANGE
Rolleston R
Hills Pk
1875
Mt Franklin
2088
West Bch
Mt Hunt
1807
Green Hill
1570
Forest Pk
1476

Mt Armstrong
2103
Mt Philistine
1951
Phipps Pk
1984
Goat Pass
Mt Valiant
1817
Castle Hill
1530
Casey
Casey Stm

Carrington Pk
2077
Summit Shelter
Mt Temple
1892
Page Shelter
Blimit
1923
Mt Oates
2009
Falling Mountain
1828
Hawdon
1984
Aeroplane Flat
Brown Hill
1714

Mt Rolleston
2271
ROME RIDGE
Mt Campbell
1844
Waimakariri River
JELLICOE RIDGE
Mt Aicken
1859
ARTHUR'S PASS
1692 Mt O'Malley
Mt Scott
1929
Mt Wilson
SAVANNAH RANGE

MAIN DIVIDE
Avalanche Pk
1753
Mt Stewart
1932
Mt Bealey
1823
Mt Williams
1713
Edwards
POLAR RANGE
The Pyramid
1615
Woolshed Hill
1431

Mt Davie
2294
CAMP SPUR
Greyneys Shelter
Dome
1939
Sudden Valley Stm
Hawdon Shelter
Andrews Shelter
Andrews Stm

White R
2240
Mt Harper
Klondyke Shelter
Bealey River

Mt Murchison
2400

Mt Gizeh
2164
WAIMAKARIRI RIVER
73
Cass
1360
Sugar Loaf
N

0   k ms   10
Mt Binser
1858

©Copyright Automobile Association.

75

The sub-alpine and alpine vegetation of the park, starting just below the snow line and extending up to the highest altitudes, is rich in variety and the flowering which occurs up here in summer is another of the park's splendours. Sub-alpine scrub includes coprosmas, snow totara, hebes and, on the western slopes, leatherwood. At higher altitudes, tussock and snowgrass, followed by alpine grasslands, take over.

Alpine vegetation is within easy reach of summer visitors. The accessibility which the park derives from highway and railway is thoroughly demonstrated by your ability to make a short climb to the roof of the park and find rare beauty spread at your feet. Here are alpine daisies, coprosmas, violets, snowberries, gentians and mountain foxgloves. There are vegetable sheep both normal and giant, a black daisy and mosses and lichens. Here too is the so-called Mt Cook lily, in fact a giant mountain buttercup which no foreign species can surpass in size or beauty. The giant vegetable sheep, its surface made up of the leafy tips of hundreds of branches packed so tightly that it is difficult to thrust a finger between them, can be large enough to be mistaken for real sheep. Up here, too, are delicately-structured alpine bogs with sedges, bog pine, pigmy pine (the world's smallest pine) and the beautiful, if unattractively-named, bog cushion, which produces copious white blossoms from a thick, dark green carpet. This world of miniature plants has a charm and variety no less than that of the deep forests and when the snow has disappeared no visitor to the park should miss the opportunity to discover this aspect of the New Zealand landscape.

Any discussion of wildlife in the park is dominated by the damage done to native tree, shrub and alpine garden by deer, opossum and chamois. The deer has been responsible for the wholesale destruction of alpine herbfields, one of the botanical wonders of the Southern Alps and high ranges elsewhere in the South Island. But all three introduced animals are an appalling menace to the park. Native bird life is varied, with both river and forest species, and insect life in the park, including a giant dragonfly, offers much of interest to the sharp-eyed.

The attractions of the park and the ease with which many people can reach it from Canterbury and Westland gives it a diversified recreational role. Walking, tramping, skiing and climbing are all well catered for and the use made of the park is reflected in almost 90 huts, bivouacs and shelters spread throughout it. Children's summer adventure camps run by the Park Board and park interpretation programmes during holidays help thousands of people each year to appreciate the beauties – and the dangers – of the park. It should be remembered that although accessible, this is high alpine country and the twin hazards of weather and exposure are never far away.

The Dobson Walk takes visitors through a fascinating world of miniature plant life, growing in alpine bog and sub-alpine scrub and herbfields. The walk provides a uniquely easy way of seeing the plant and insect life which exists high up in the Southern Alps.

A snow gentian *(Gentiana corymbifera)* finds a place among other alpine plants on a ledge.

Pleasant walking amongst alpine herbfields.

This buttercup *(Ranuculus haastii)* is a remarkable species of its kind, being restricted to the bare and unstable shingle screes of the South Island. Its smooth and fleshy leaves are only a few centimetres high and die down before winter.

T. Pitman

The large mountain daisy *(Celmisia coriacea)* is a striking representative of the New Zealand daisy family, many members of which are unique to this country. Its upright habit is distinctive. Some 60 species of *Celmisia* are found only in New Zealand and some regard this as the finest of them all.

T. Pitman

The huge scree slopes of Arthur's Pass are typical of those throughout the Southern Alps. They seem on first glance to be devoid of life and incapable of sustaining it. But nature is full of surprises and this daisy *(Cotula atrata)* is one of the select group of plants equipped to survive here.

The Temple Basin skifields.

Arthur's Pass National Park has taught many New Zealand climbers their first skills. Mt Murchison and Mt Harper (right) are part of the extensive invitation which the park offers to those who want to test themselves against conditions on the roof of New Zealand.

There is organised skiing in the Temple Basin area by the pass summit and the Park Board has a firm policy of controlling development here to protect wilderness qualities. Temple Basin provides tremendous views of the Southern Alps and the ranges of Westland and is worth the trek in summer or winter for casual visitors. There is plenty of climbing in the park although the loose rock must be treated with care and mountaineering fatalities are not uncommon. There is fishing, too, for brown trout and quinnat salmon.

Tramping is one of the most rewarding activities in the park, with an extensive valley and river system winding between high peaks. There are tramping routes across the main divide to reveal the two-sided aspect of the park and there are innumerable routes along the sides of the mountains above the bushline. The Otehake wilderness area, which includes lovely Lake Kaurapataka, is a special attraction. Less dedicated people will find many relatively easy walks off the main highway, including the Dobson nature walk, by the memorial cairn to the discoverer of the pass. It shows off glacial moraine, reflective tarns, views of the mountains and Otira Gorge and sub-alpine scrub and herbfields. The Daisy Flat track to the Bealey River takes you to a good swimming and picnicking place from which you can see stone walling built for the old coach road. The Devils Punchbowl Falls, the Bridal Veil walk and longer walks into the upper Otira and Bealey valleys all offer their own individual contribution to enjoyment of the park.

To simply travel through Arthur's Pass as a way of crossing the Southern Alps is to respond to the massive beauty of this landscape. Yet beyond the confines of gorge and river valley through which highway and railway pass there is a national park with many faces, moods, invitations and challenges. It lies astride a famous New Zealand alpine crossing which has its own drama, but it is also a park which would have earned a worthy reputation even if young Arthur Dobson had never pointed a road in its direction.

Arthurs Pass National Park

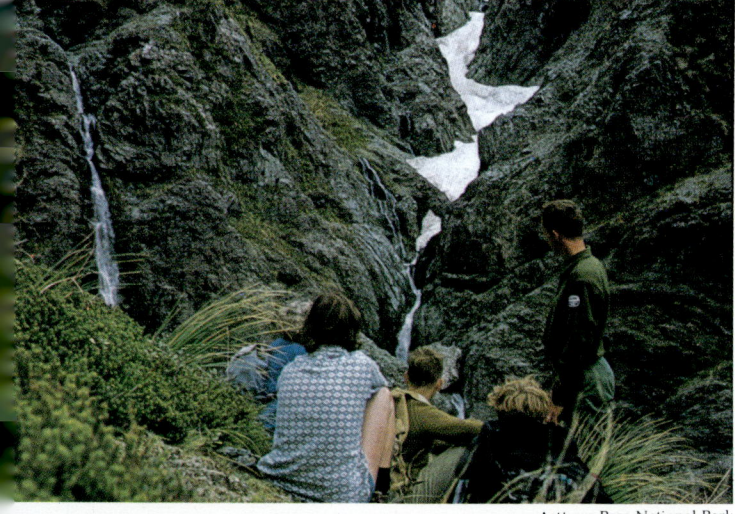

Park rangers make any walk an instructive experience and invest what you see with a meaning which may otherwise not be apparent. Here a ranger discusses the glacial history of the park with a party above a tongue of the Bealey Glacier.

The korimako, or bellbird, is one of the New Zealand forest's most beautiful choristers, its notes as liquid as the nectar on which it feeds. It is the concert master of the dawn chorus which makes the New Zealand bush resound in a way which held spellbound the early European explorers. Early risers will hear it in the bush of this park.

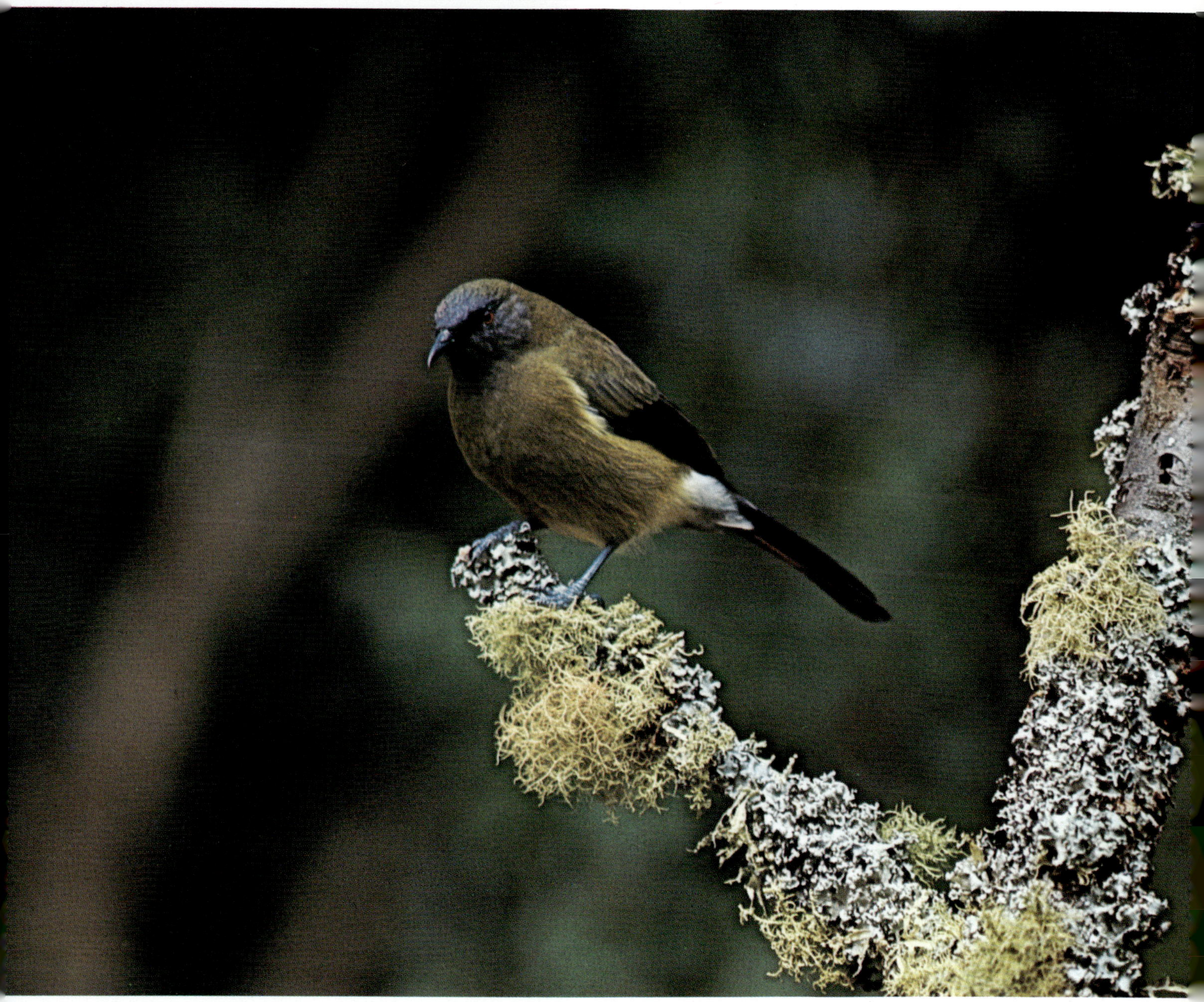

G. Moon

Westland National Park

In Westland National Park, the Southern Alps stretch fingers of ice towards the sea in a cold caress which has no parallel in nature.

Two great glaciers spill from frozen mountain peaks down deep valleys where a rain forest stands higher than the glistening rivers of ice. Nowhere else in the world's temperate zones do glaciers thrust so close to sea level. The contrast between the blue-white masses of moving ice and the forest which grows thickly near them is unforgettable. Above, the rearing mountains overwhelm all else.

To most visitors, Westland National Park is the Franz Josef and Fox Glaciers. It is natural for them to dominate impressions of this part of New Zealand for they are both dramatic and accessible. Where else can you, within minutes of leaving your car, be walking in summer clothes on the broken face of a glacier?

Yet this park is much more than glaciers. It is the soaring mountains, high snow fields, deep forest, alpine herbfields, rushing streams and waterfalls, winding rivers, hot springs, still lakes – all of the natural variety of which New Zealand is capable. This variety arises from the character of the park, which is unique among our national parks in rising from sea level to 3498 m – the peak of beautiful Mt Tasman, second highest mountain in New Zealand. Snow and rock wastes seen against forests of subtropical luxuriance and a virtually untouched wilderness area within the park's boundaries give this land a rare immunity from man's works.

Gold first brought Europeans here in significant numbers and as it petered out, the glaciers and mountains became the focus for travellers from the early 1900s. Gold helped to found the fortunes of the Graham family, who later played a prominent part in the development of West Coast tourism and recognition of the

A tarn reflects the beginning of a new day in Westland as Mt Cook (right) and Mt Tasman, New Zealand's highest peaks, peep over the foothills of the Southern Alps. Tall kahikatea trees add another essential ingredient to the mixture which proclaims the essence of Westland National Park.

The splendour of the Southern Alps from Westland. Mt Cook (right) and Mt Tasman dominate the other peaks, but all of the highest mountains here are above 3000 m. The forces which shaped the land are strikingly evident in the steep western scarp of the mountains and the immense size of the moraines left in the foreground by advances of the glaciers during the coldest part of the Ice Age more than 17,000 years ago. Lake Mueller and its small companion fill basins left on the top of the moraine by retreating ice.

unique Franz Josef and Fox Glaciers. Tourism has passed from the glory of the splendid old wooden hotel of the Grahams at Franz Josef, where leisurely resort holidays were once the style, to a more hurried kind of tourism which sees guests arrive one day and speed on their way the next, satisfied by a walk on the glaciers or even merely a view of them. The opening of the Haast highway in 1965 to make a through route across the Southern Alps between Westland and Otago has made the difference.

But the park has abundant rewards for those who take time to explore it more fully. No national park is more varied in relation to size. None is better served by its approach roads, passing under the wall of the mountains and through tremendous stands of native forest which simply by their beauty crystallise arguments against continued logging of this national asset. The height of the trees is an apt introduction to the natural extravagances found in the park. Lakes are visible reminders that this is glacier country and then you cross milky rivers with thin mist writhing over them to signal the presence close by of the immense glaciers.

The milky colour is your first glimpse of the living power of the glaciers because it comes from the grinding together of ice and rock during their journey out of the mountains. The mist, which gave the name Waiho – 'smoking water' – to the Franz Josef Glacier river, is caused by contact between the cold water and the warmer, moist air. Follow the rivers by road and they take you into those deep, cloud-roofed valleys of ice.

After the Maori, who were scattered only sparsely through Westland, came Tasman, whose memorable log entry, 'Towards the middle of the day we saw a great land uplifted high,' recorded his discovery of New Zealand on December 13, 1642. The snows of the Southern Alps somewhere near the park signalled Tasman's discovery but he saw no glaciers. Neither did Cook, who in 1774 dismissed the area as unworthy of observation, describing it as 'wild, craggy and desolate.' Thomas Brunner was apparently not aware of the two huge glaciers so close by during his famous journey from Nelson to Paringa and back in 1846-48.

The first published description came from Francis and Young on the brig *Mary Louisa* , whose log for June 14, 1859, read in part: 'At noon, abreast of Mt Cook, close in shore, we could see distinctly that it was an immense field of ice, entirely filling up the valley formed by the spurs of the twin peaks and running far down into the low land. It was a pale green colour and appeared to be quite a mile in width towards the lower end of the valley.'

From the Alex Knob track there is a view of the whole length of the Franz Josef Glacier spilling its ice down the steep western scarp of the Southern Alps. Precipitous valley walls show the scars of centuries of grinding ice. On the right a trim line in the vegetation is clearly visible. Below the terminal face of the glacier, the Waiho River begins its winding course through rock and gravel deposited by the glacier in ages past.

At that time the glaciers were more than 2 km closer to the sea than they are today.

In the year following that sighting, the Ngai Tahu sold to the Crown more than 3 million ha of land stretching from western Nelson to Milford Sound and inland to the main divide of the Southern Alps. It included what is now the park, which was a scenic reserve for many years before becoming a national park on March 29, 1960, as part of the celebration of Westland's centenary.

This 'land uplifted high' is the result of enormous land-building forces. Running through the middle of the park parallel with the coast is the New Zealand alpine fault, the largest fault in the country and one of the most significant in the world. It runs for about 600 km in an almost straight line from Marlborough to Milford Sound and out into the Tasman Sea. Pressure at this tear in the earth's crust has forced land on one side of the fault to move both horizontally and vertically against land on the other. The vertical movement has created the Southern Alps. In a sense, it has created much of the South Island, for the narrow plains to the west of the mountains and the broad plains to the east have been built from material eroded off the high peaks over tens of thousands of years.

The land to the east of the fault began thrusting up about 150 million years ago and the main uplift occurred during the last five million years. The mountains rose much faster than erosion, even the glacial erosion of the Ice Age, could wear them down. They are, with their very steep western scarp and rugged terrain, a classic example of mountain-building by faulting. Their sharp uplift and their effect on the weather has given us the unique Fox and Franz Josef Glaciers.

The rock which was raised to form the mountains was originally mud and sand lying under the sea and was profoundly altered more than 150 million years ago when it was deeply buried in the earth and folded by movement of the planet's crust. Intense heat and pressure created new minerals and arranged them in parallel bands which give the rock a tendency to split into thin layers. Called schist, from the Greek skhistos (to split), the banded arrangement is shown along the glacier valley walls where ice has planed the rock smooth. The complex folding which took place varied from the tiny proportions seen in small rocks littering the valley floors below the glaciers to huge folds 3-5 km across in the surrounding country.

Rock to the west of the fault is perhaps 500 to 600 million years old and is possibly the oldest in New Zealand. To the east, it is about 200 to 300 million years old. Along the fault, the rock is severely crushed and shattered by aeons of pressure and grinding – a process which continues today. The line of the fault is difficult to see from the ground but is clearly visible from the air. Just south of the Waikukupa River, the main highway between Franz Josef and Fox passes through distinctive blue-green rock which is right on the fault and has been shattered by movement along it.

Everywhere in the park are signs of what the glaciers have done to the landscape since mountain-building ended. During the Ice Age, which lasted more than a million years, the extent and movement of glaciers out of the high regions of the South Island was tremendous. The land bears their imprint in lakes and scooped out valleys, some of them drowned by the sea as in Fiordland. The Ice Age consisted of many periods of extreme coldness, or glaciations, interspersed with periods of warmth similar to today's climate. The glaciers advanced and retreated accordingly and the last glaciation, between 14,000 and 16,000 years ago, carried the Franz Josef and Fox Glaciers beyond the present coastline, some 19 km from where their terminal faces are today. During the coldest glaciations, ice sheets covered the whole coastal lowland of the park.

Advances and retreats continue today as the glaciers respond to short and long term weather influences but on a smaller scale because of the relatively stable climate now current. Since the first European records, the trend has been retreat, interrupted by advances which have never recovered all of the ground lost.

The story of the glaciers starts high in the Southern Alps and far out over the Tasman Sea. The mountains are so close to the sea that the prevailing westerly winds which hit them are still full of moisture which they dump heavily and often as rain and snow. Near the park coastline, average annual rainfall is more than 3000 mm, rising to between 4000 and 5000 mm in the alpine foothills and close to 8000 mm in the mountains, most of it falling as snow higher up. Yearly snowfall in the névés, or snow fields, which feed the Franz Josef and Fox Glaciers is thought to be as much as 60 to 90 m. Here then are the conditions which have created more than 60 named glaciers in Westland National Park.

Franz Josef and Fox are by far the largest on the western side of the alpine divide, but another 29 in the park are classed as large or secondary. They are suspended much higher up in the mountains, with their terminal faces about 900 m above sea level, compared with about 300 m for Franz Josef and 260 m for Fox. All of them have shrunk considerably in recent times and some have been cut off from their snow fields and are fed mainly by avalanche snow falling on them from the rims of their valley walls.

Up in the permanent snowfields of the Southern Alps, the glaciers have their beginning. This is the Névé of Franz Josef Glacier. It provides the snow and ice which is the glacier's raw material and the steep western face of the Southern Alps is the glacier's staircase. These snowfields may be up to 900 m deep and those of the Franz Josef and Fox Glaciers are the largest on the western side of the Southern Alps.

A legacy of the glaciers of long ago, Lake Mapourika mirrors podocarp forest while the Southern Alps shine between morning cloud.

The power of moving ice has created the fantastic, pinnacle-shaped upthrusts in the main icefall of Fox Glacier. At left, the ice is coloured by rock debris, or morainic material, testifying also to the energy of the glacier.

The snow fields which feed the Fox and Franz Josef Glaciers are much the biggest on the western side of the Southern Alps. They accumulate huge masses of snow which are estimated to be as deep as 900 m in places. The Fox snow field has a catchment area of about 3200 ha and that of the Franz Josef is about 2000 ha. The extent and capacity of the snow fields, high precipitation and the steep western scarp of the mountains are the factors which drive the two glaciers so far down their valleys.

It is difficult to conceive the strength of the forces which make solid ice flow as glaciers. The change from snow to ice occurs as the weight of succeeding snowfalls packs the lower layers tighter and tighter, driving out trapped air, until the crystals at the lower levels fuse and become a solid mass of clear ice. About 20 m of snow are required to produce clear ice. As more snow falls on top of this dense mass, the pressure on the ice below becomes so great that it distorts the structure of the ice molecules and they begin to slip against one another. Some 45 m of snow and ice are believed to be required before the ice will flow and a glacier is born.

As the glacier ice moves down its valley, it collects rock debris falling on it from erosion of the valley walls above by water, frost and ice and grinds other rock from the walls and floor to carry it along. The debris is called morainic material and you can see it discolouring the glacier right down to the terminal face. Glaciers flow as rivers do, faster in the middle than at the sides and bottom, where friction contributes to the tumbling action which grinds up morainic material into the fine 'rock flour' which colours glacial rivers.

The glaciers in the park, whose inland boundary is the main divide, flow faster than those on the other side because the western valleys are steeper. The upper limits of the Franz Josef and Fox snow fields are about 2700 m above sea level and the glaciers fall some 2400 m from there to their terminal faces. That fall occurs over a distance of 13 km with the Fox and 11 km with the Franz Josef. The overall gradient of each is about the same, close to 200 m in each kilometre, but the Franz Josef flows faster because its tongue – that part between the bottom lip of the snow field and the terminal face – is steeper, dropping about 250 m in each kilometre compared with 150 m on the Fox. Both glaciers travel at up to about 2 m a day.

A glacier's journey ends where its tongue melts at the same rate as the ice is flowing downhill. You can watch the process and it is by no means gentle. Great chunks of ice regularly thump down from the terminal faces around their ice caves formed by the rivers emerging from the glaciers. The rivers start high up on the glaciers and are fed by melting ice, rain and streams from the valley walls.

Where glaciers turn slowly to water: The terminal faces of the Franz Josef (upper left) and Fox Glaciers reach closer to sea level than any others in the world's temperate zones. Above is the stony bed of moraine through which the Fox River runs its icy course.

Water and ice compose a picture of irresistable forces slowly wearing down the great rock uplift of the Southern Alps. The figures on the Fox Glacier give scale to the scene. The waterfall is plunging down from the valley wall and the glacier is moving left to right and down across the picture.

D. DeGray

A walk on Franz Josef or Fox Glaciers brings thousands of people to Westland National Park every year.

A terminal face shifts up and down its valley according to climatic changes and both the Franz Josef and Fox Glaciers respond to these changes unusually quickly because they are steep and push down to a comparatively warm altitude. The steeper gradient of the Franz Josef makes it particularly sensitive and its advances and retreats, closely monitored since the beginning of this century, have aroused strong interest in New Zealand and around the world.

The glacier cargo of morainic material deposited by the melting face forms what are called moraines and the valleys of both big glaciers have a number of moraines which record advances and retreats over thousands of years. They are especially well revealed from the air but visitors who first take a little time to study the glaciers in Park Board literature and the Franz Josef and Fox visitor centres can appreciate them from road and track viewpoints.

An ice cave lets visitors peek into the interior of a glacier.

Moraines and other evidence indicate that the last major glacial advances took place between 14,000 and 16,000 years ago, when the Franz Josef travelled as far as the northern end of Lake Mapourika and out into the sea. Soon after, the Ice Age began coming to an end and the glaciers started their retreat. The climate became warmer than it is now and the glaciers shrank far back into their alpine valleys, the smaller ones probably disappearing completely and the two large ones withdrawing into their snow fields. This disposes of a common misconception that the Fox and Franz Josef Glaciers are remnants of the Ice Age. They have been of course, perpetually self-renewing since then. Their various advances and retreats left behind large depressions as ice melted and these were either filled with river gravels or became lakes, lakes like Mapourika, largest in the park, Matheson, with its famous reflections of the Southern Alps, and Mueller, Gault and Wahapo.

Around 1200, the climate cooled and the glaciers advanced again until a short retreat occurred from 1600. A further advance followed until about 1750, when the climate began to move towards its present pattern and the glaciers began to fall back to their present positions.

The most distinctive moraine left by the glaciers is the Waiho Loop, an almost perfect quarter circle lying across alluvial flats 4 km northwest of Franz Josef township. It marks the furthest point to which Franz Josef Glacier advanced about 11,000 years ago, when its terminal face would have been 4 km wide, compared with less than 30 m today. The main highway crosses the eastern end of the moraine at Stony Creek, north of Franz Josef. The Tatare Stream cuts through it further south and the southern half of what was originally a semi-circle has been destroyed by the meandering Waiho River. Although the glacier advance which formed the Waiho Loop was minor when set against the last Ice Age glaciation, it was much more significant than the advances which followed in the upper Waiho Valley during the last few thousand years.

The Waiho Loop is a terminal moraine and a series of these are easily identifiable in the upper Waiho and Fox Valleys and date from the advances which came to a halt in 1600, 1750 and 1825. The moraine walk at Fox Glacier takes you over material deposited by the first two advances.

Lateral moraines are formed of material deposited along the sides of the glaciers. There is a good example on the southwestern side of the lower Waiho Valley which was deposited during the last Ice Age glaciation. It is about 150m high. A moraine of similar age between the Waiho Loop and the sea shows just how massive was the carving of rock from the mountains during the last glaciation. Other moraines of various shapes and sizes wind over the park lowlands and the road to Gillespies Beach demonstrates the irregular topography, while at the beach itself is a big lateral moraine deposited when Fox Glacier was melting into the sea. The high valley walk at Fox Glacier lets you put your feet on what the glacier has wrought because it crosses the park's best example of a series of lateral moraines. Formed like giant steps are seven benches carved out by successive drops in the level of glacier ice with intervening periods of relative climatic stability.

The weather and the mountains make the glaciers of Westland National Park and the glaciers quarry the rock which forms the river bed in the foreground, an endless cycle. This view of the Waiho River again emphasises the contrasts found within Westland National Park.

Lake Gault lies between two moraines of different ages and a track to the lake crosses one of them. The top of the moraine is level with the height the ice once reached, more than 150 m above the nearby river flats and is an impressive demonstration of Ice Age conditions 16,000 years ago. The lake gives more panoramic reflections of the Southern Alps than Lake Matheson. Both lakes have the dark brown water, derived from the leaching of forest humus, which give the lakes their reflective properties.

Glaciers leave other marks. In the Fox and Franz Josef valleys below the terminal faces are roches moutonée, or sheep-like rocks, sculpted by ice flowing over them in earlier times. They have been smoothed on the upstream side by ice riding over them and 'plucked' on the downstream side by ice freezing to the rock and pulling away fragments as it moves on. Sentinel Rock at Franz Josef and Cone Rock at Fox are the biggest of them and ice once rose to the top of the latter, 277 m above the river.

Below the Fox Glacier are large mounds of dead ice, so named because it is ice which has become detached from the moving glacier. Dead ice is often covered by rock debris which prevents it from melting except very slowly. Masses of dead ice around Cone Rock have been there for many decades and some carry a thick carpet of scrub. Below them is a carpet of morainic gravel and underneath that again is a basin filled with centuries-old ice. The melting of dead ice leaves water-filled depressions called kettlehole lakes – miniature versions of the park's larger lakes formed by the same process. Peters Pool at Franz Josef Glacier is one and there are others below both terminal faces. A ' glacier mill' – a deep hole carved in a valley wall by the whirlpool action of ice – can be seen at Franz Josef.

Forest on the valley walls tells its own story through 'trim lines' marking the effect of glacier fluctuations on the trees. A trim line from the 1750 advance, 275 m above the river bed, shows how much ice once filled the valley. Trees which grew below the trim line after the glacier receded are markedly smaller than those above. Further down towards the sea, dating of vegetation reveals a tale of forest establishing itself on land vacated by the glaciers, only to be mown down again by subsequent advances of ice. The rata which makes a brilliant display of red blossom against the mountains in summer was the leading colonist with its tiny, easily-windblown seeds and is a major inhabitant of the park's forests.

Plants colonise morainic material below the Franz Josef Glacier.

An alpine rock daisy (*Celmisia walkeri*) sprouts from a sheer wall of schist at Franz Josef Glacier. The schist, with its parallel arrangement of minerals in thin bands, has been planed down by glacier ice which once covered it.

D. DeGrav

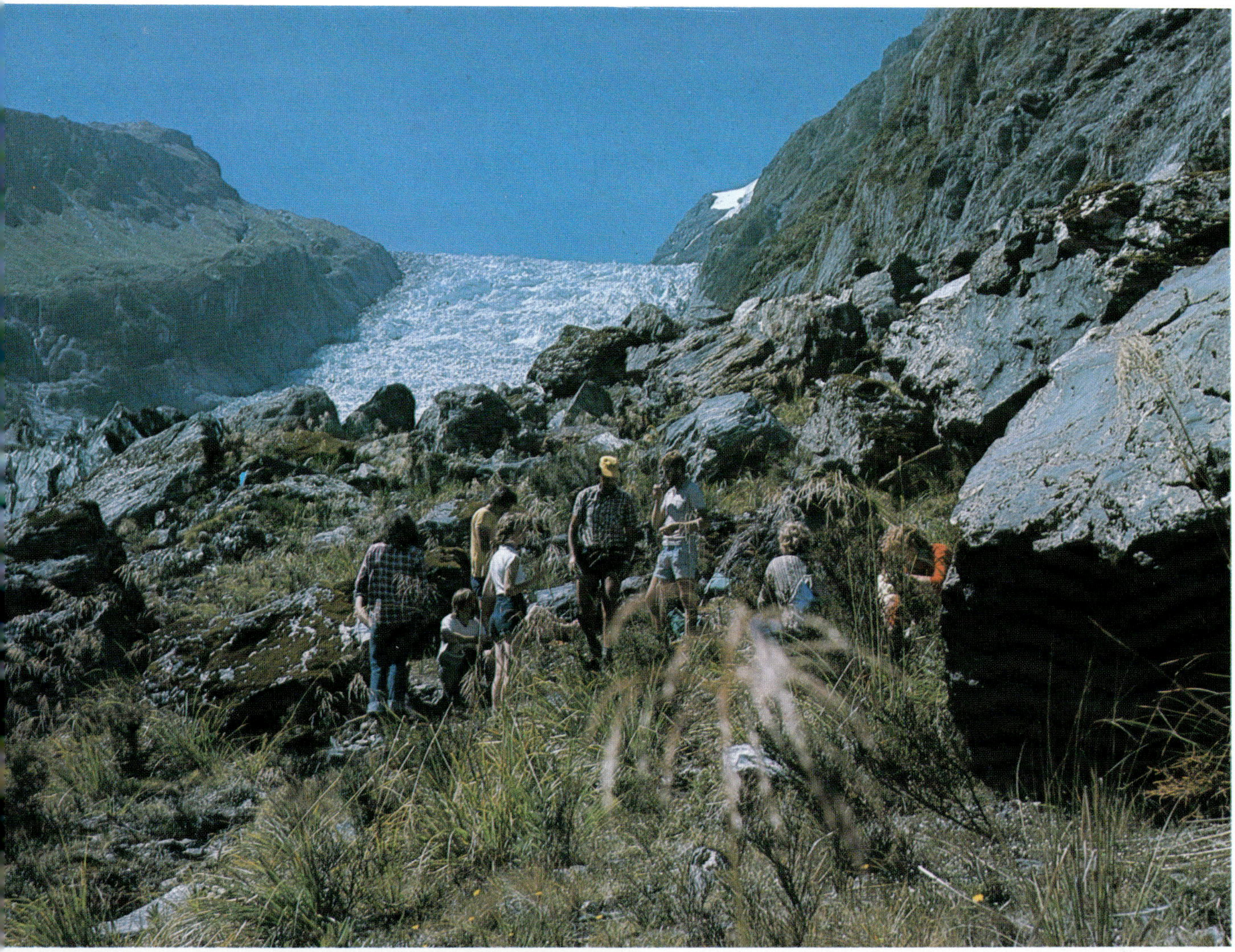

Alpine grassland thrives above the glistening ice of Fox Glacier, allowing a guided party to appreciate the infinite variety of nature.

The inquisitive and friendly toutouwai, or South Island robin. You will come to know it well in the national parks of the South Island.

The little mountain heath *(Pentachondra pumila)* brightens many of the park's tracks and nature walks with its berries.

T. Pitman

T. Pitman

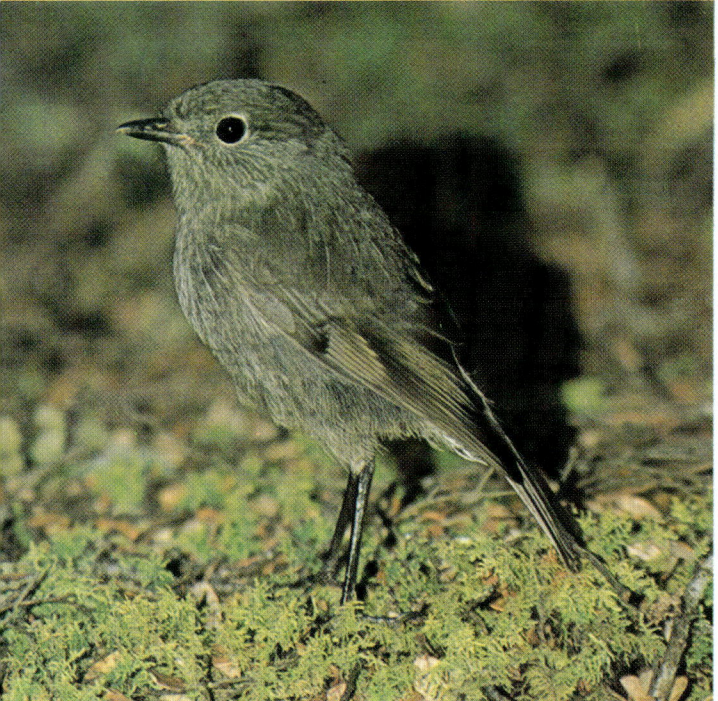

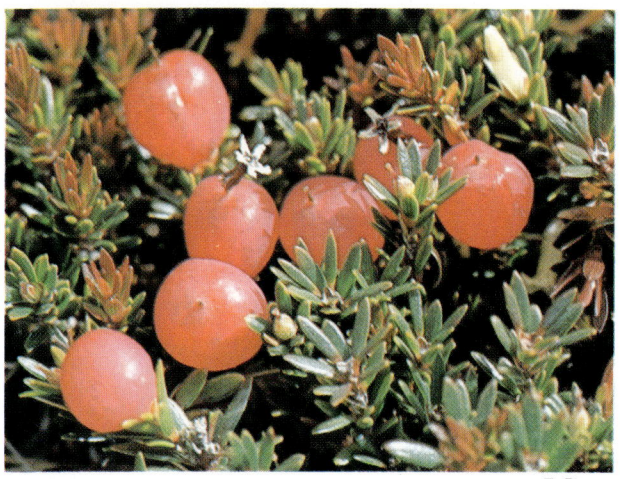

The magnificent Southern Alps, the long ridge which parts the sky of Aotearoa.

Okarito

Okarito Lagoon

L'Wahapo

WHATAROA

Lake Mapourika

Tatare

FRANZ JOSEF

Docherty Ck

Waiho River

Waikukupa River

L Gault   L Mueller

L Matheson

1295   Alex Knob

Callery

Crawford Knob
1821

FRITZ   RANGE

Franz Josef Glacier

Almer   Geikie
Snowfield

Elie de Beaumont
3116

Mt Walter 2903

Mt Green 2850

2822 Hochstetter Dome

DIVIDE

2444 Mt Frances

Grey Gl

Godley Glacier

Mt D'Archiac
2865

MAIN

Classen Gl

Cook River   Fox   River

6

FOX GLACIER

1022 Mt Fox

Fox

Fox Gl

Chancellor Dome
1989

Chancellor

2665 De la Beche
Mt Halcombe

Minarets 3055
2992

Tasman Saddle

Mannering 2637

Godley River

Karangarua

Craig Creek

FOX

RANGE

Balfour Gl

Albert Glacier

Pioneer

Douglas Pk
3085

Mt Haidinger
3066

Mt Haast 3138

Mt Tasman 3498

Mt Hamilton
3155

Malte Brun

Mt Chudleigh
2952

MT COOK NATIONAL PARK

Mt Ronald Adair 2812

Mt Hutton 2850

MALTE BRUN RANGE

Murchison Glacier

La Perouse Gl

1943 Ryan Pk NAVIGATOR

Mt Copland
RA 2346

La Perouse
3079

Mt Hicks Mt Dampier
3216   3440

3764
Mt Cook

Haast

Tasman Glacier

Nazomi
2911

Ball

Gardner

LIEBIG RANGE

Murchison River

WESTLAND NATIONAL PARK

Strauchon Gl

Copland River

Welcome Flat
Springs

Mt Vexation
1661

Douglas Rock

The Footstool
2765

Douglas Neve

Mt Sefton 3157

Mt Brunner 2667

Copland Shelter
Hooker

Sefton Biv

MAIN   DIVIDE

Hooker Gl

BALL HUT RD

HOOKER RA

MT COOK RA

Douglas R

Mt Peculiar
1844

Douglas

Gardner

N

Mt Mueller

Hunters
Haven

HERMITAGE

Mt Isabel 2596

Mueller Glacier

MAIN DIVIDE

TASMAN RIVER

Fettes Pk
2454

HOOKER RANGE

Mt Darby Mt Sealy
2526   2637

80

0   kms   10

©Copyright Automobile Association.

92

The differences in altitude and soil types within the park have given rise to a diverse range of vegetation. Kahikatea thrives in the swampy lowlands while the better-drained soils support totara, matai and many other less prominent species. Glacial terraces between the hill country and the sea have for main vegetation a mixed podocarp forest, mainly of rimu but also with miro, kahikatea and rata. The hill country below the mountains supports rata, kamahi, Hall's totara, miro and rimu, some of the last being extremely tall and ancient. Rata-kamahi forest is the main type of tree on the lower mountain slopes, giving way to smaller vegetation as altitude increases.

A track to the top of Alex Knob at Franz Josef takes you up through most of the successive plant types in the park, from rain forest with its struggling undergrowth to sub-alpine scrub, snow grasses and mountain flowers at the highest level. From the top of this rock and also from Cone Rock at Fox Glacier there are views of the entire glaciers, some 300 km of coastline and of ancient glacial features on the coastal plains.

Opportunities for walking, tramping or mountaineering abound in Westland National Park. There are 21 short walks suitable for most people and the park has plenty of scope for the tramper, whether you like exploring heavy bush, coastal beaches and lagoons or high river valleys. You can see a colony of fur seals at Gillespies Beach, which hundreds of people once worked for gold, but keep your distance and approach quietly. They are the only species of seal which breed on the New Zealand mainland and thoughtless visitors may place this colony in danger.

The mountains loom over the park with a grandeur irresistible to the eye – and the ambitions of climbers. Mountaineering has been one of the prime recreational activities in the park area since the 1880s, when a string of first ascents began. The unpredictable weather of Westland, the heavy rainfall and the steep western faces of the alpine peaks issue a tough challenge to climbers. Tomorrow might bring a fine day made for climbing, but it might bring a westerly roaring in from the Tasman Sea to throw a blizzard fit and pen climbers in their huts. One of the mountain huts is the highest building in New Zealand. This is Pioneer Hut, 2600 m above sea level, standing under Douglas Peak at the head of the Fox Glacier snow field, looking as though only sheer determination holds it there.

A double crossing of the main alpine divide by Grahams Saddle and Copland Pass is the park's finest mountaineering trip and there is a warm pool at Welcome Flat in the Copland Valley to minister to climbers. Ski planes are now often used to get into remote places before the climbing begins. A scenic flight on one of these aircraft, with a landing on one of the glacier snowfields, is

The road to Gillespies Beach passes through a wide range of native forest, with ferns and many other ground plants blanketing the forest floor.

New Zealand's helmet orchids are among the native orchids which have the biggest number of species. This is *Pterostylis banksii*.

T. Pitman

The tangled bush of Westland National Park is a profusion of trees, mosses, ferns, climbers and perchers, a living web which encourages the use of tracks.

The forest floor of wet Westland is drenched with an immense variety of plants.

an excellent introduction to the park. They are reasonably innocuous in the park wilderness but the same cannot be said of the helicopters joyriding tourists up the Fox Valley for a quick landing on the glacier. They beat an intrusive note into a raw, rugged area in which people should be allowed to contemplate, even wonder at, nature's implacable ways without modern mechanical interference.

When visiting this park, remember that it is in a region of rain forest and that rainfall is frequent and often heavy. Be prepared for it. Without the rain, the park would not have many of the characteristics which make it so magnificent. In summer the mountains tend to cloud over during the day, so that the early mornings and late afternoons are the best times to view them. Winter often provides clear, fine days. When it is cloudy inland it is often fine on the coast and it is well to be flexible in your approach to the park.

It pays dividends to visit the Park Board's headquarters at Franz Josef township early in your visit. It has one of the most comprehensive visitor centres in the national parks system and its well-produced displays will arm you with useful information for understanding the many features of the park.

In a park of such diversity, no visitor will go away without having achieved a measure of pleasure and satisfaction. It is one of the most remarkable places in the world and perhaps unique in having such a complete record of glacial and climatic cycles in the few kilometres between the mighty Southern Alps and the Tasman Sea.

Snow, sky and man – the call of high places.
D. Lowe

Mount Cook National Park

Training ground for the New Zealander who first conquered Mt Everest and one of the world's most beautiful and massive mountain chains, the Southern Alps graze the New Zealand sky for more than 400 km.

Their long plateau of jagged summits, rising steeply from forest and plain and fixed fast in winter by snow and ice, give the South Island a scenic dimension which borders on the extravagant. The mountains seem over-generous in height compared with the slenderness of the land.

The Southern Alps reach their apotheosis in Mt Cook, the highest mountain in New Zealand and the starting point for every New Zealander's geography lessons. Topping 3764 m, sheer-sided and sharply ridged, it stands clear of neighbouring Mt Tasman by a margin of 264 m.

The mountain is the genesis of Mt Cook National Park but many other great mountains shoulder it because this is an area of massive alpine features. More than a third of the park is covered by permanent snow and the creeping ice of large glaciers. It rises from plains built of cubic kilometres of glacier-carried rock to the main divide of the Southern Alps, where its western rim meets Westland National Park. Along that meeting line are New Zealand's highest mountains, the culmination of the great upthrust which created the Southern Alps.

Above all rises Mt Cook, the point to which your eyes return again and again.

The Maori name for the mountain, Aorangi, is popularly translated as Cloud Piercer, but this is not the real meaning of the name. The direct translation is Cloud in the Sky (ao: cloud; rangi: sky) and there are, as with many Maori names, several versions of how the name arose. One is that the mountain was named after peaks in the Cook and Society Islands which the Maori came to know during their voyages down to New Zealand.

The south face of Mt Cook demonstrates why Mt Cook National Park has larger areas of permanent snowfield than any comparable region outside the polar circles.

Another version, more romantic, says that the crew of the great Araitiuru canoe, which came from the Maori's ancestral land Hawaiki in the 14th Century and was wrecked on the South Island coast, travelled north towards the Southern Alps, naming mountains as they went. When they saw that Mt Cook was the highest, they thought to name it after the tallest member of their party. This was a small boy named Aorangi, who was being carried on his grandfather's shoulders.

Another and older story is that Aorangi was the captain of the canoe Te Waka-a-Aorangi (the Canoe of Aorangi), which brought to an earth inhabited by the gods the children of the sky. It was turned into stone and Aorangi became Mt Cook. His three brothers were turned into Mounts Dampier, Teichelmann and the Silberhorn.

Mountains shrink your human stature here. The only way over that is to climb them. Within the park or along the ranges which form its boundaries are 19 principal peaks more than 3000 m high and half as many minor peaks again above this height. Only a few New Zealand mountains above 3000 m are found outside Mt Cook National Park. The high reach of the park is further emphasised by the fact that it has about 150 peaks higher than 2000 m in its 64 km length.

Mountains do not, though, provide all of the Park's alpine essence. There is also the Tasman Glacier, 28 km long and up to 3 km or more wide, one of the largest in the world outside the polar regions. And the Godley, Classen, Murchison and Mueller Glaciers, all of them notable ice flows by any standard. There are a number of hanging glaciers perched high up in the mountains, spending themselves in constant avalanches, and bigger snowfields than any comparable area in the world outside the Himalayas and the Arctic and Antarctic.

The geology which underlies the steep topography of the Southern Alps is described in the Westland chapter, but in Mt Cook National Park there are remarkable examples of the process of mountain building and erosion. The road approaches to the park are across plains which have been built by glaciers bringing rock down out of the mountains over tens of thousands of years. The Tasman and Godley Glaciers extended beyond the outlets of Lakes Pukaki and Tekapo respectively during the coldest phases, or glaciations, of the Ice Age. As they retreated, their previous paths were filled with water to form the lakes.

Mountain and glacier form a visual partnership of great beauty. This view of Mt Cook shows the steepness of the Hochstetter Glacier icefall. To the right is the hanging Freshfield Glacier, which loses its ice by avalanche on to the Tasman Glacier, and further right still is the Haast Glacier.

The milky blue of Lake Pukaki reveals the glacial origin of its waters. The main glaciers of the park drain into the lake, in which is suspended the fine 'rock flour' of meltwater from glacier ice. Beyond the tussock country rise the mountains of the park's southern boundary.

Morning shadows creep down the mighty bulk of New Zealand's highest mountains, Mt Cook (3764 m) on the left and Mt Tasman (3500 m). Below them plunges the beautiful Hochstetter Glacier, often called an icefall because of its steepness, and to the left is the Ball Glacier, both of them on their way to join the Tasman Glacier. To the left of Ball Glacier is a striking example of an old lateral moraine, now cut by erosion, left by the Tasman Glacier.

The Minarets, both about 3050 m high, stand out above Ranfurly Glacier, which flows down on to the top part of the Tasman Glacier. This photograph illustrates the masses of snow which eventually form the dense ice of the glaciers.

Mt Hamilton (2994 m), second highest peak in the Malte Brun Range of the park. The Murchison Glacier lies at the foot of the break in the mountains behind.

The upper slope of the Tasman Glacier seen from the Malte Brun hut. Mt Elie de Beaumont (3116 m) and Mt Green (2849 m) are on the left and the snowy pile of Hochstetter Dome (2821 m) is on the right. The glacier curves to the right in front of Hochstetter Dome towards its head and the Tasman Saddle.

Behind the climber on Glacier Dome, the Tasman Glacier sweeps down from its snowfields. Below Mt De La Beche (2992 m), the Rudolph Glacier runs down to join its larger sister.

At the foot of the Tasman Glacier lie huge mounds of dead, or black, ice covered with debris collected on the glacier's journey down from the mountains. It is a testament to the attack by water, wind and temperature on the great peaks.

The red rock slabs of Malte Brun (3154 m) angle their way up to Cheval Ridge, a favourite target for climbers. The inclined strata of the rock is a result of the enormous folding of land which occurred during the building of the Southern Alps. The Malte Brun Range provides some of the best rock climbing in the park.

Each of the glacier advances laid down huge carpets of rock and gravel. The points they reached before retreating again are shown in low hills, set among the plains, which are built of the debris piled up by the glacier snouts. The plains are also built of this debris, levelled by river action and the rock-breaking effects of very cold temperatures. These beds of rock may be as much as 300-400 m deep. A moraine left by the Tasman Glacier at the Birch Hill Stream several thousand years ago is crossed by the road to the Hermitage, about 6.5 km down from the hotel.

Another sign of the power of glaciers is the milky colours of Lakes Pukaki and Tekapo, caused by the 'rock flour' which is produced from the grinding together of ice and rock during a glacier's journey. During the Ice Age glaciations, the Tasman Glacier surface was many hundreds of metres higher than the Hermitage, which is itself 760 m above sea level. Even today, the ice of the glacier is estimated to be up to 600 m thick.

Although Mt Cook National Park was not founded until 1953, much of its 70,000 ha area was reserved for recreation from as early as 1885, a year after the first of the three Hermitage Hotels had opened for business. National attention was focussed on the region after Julius Haast, later knighted by both Queen Victoria and Emperor Franz Josef of Austria to become Sir Julius von Haast, visited Mt Cook in 1862 as geologist to the Canterbury Provincial Government.

Haast's description of the area may have attracted an English climber, the Rev. W. S. Green, accompanied by two Swiss mountaineers, Emil Boss and Ulrich Kaufman, to make the first attempt to climb Mt Cook in 1882. Struggling with the rough ground as well as pathfinding, they came very close to success, but after spending a night near the summit apparently could not summon the strength to make the final half-hour climb. With the establishment of the hotel and then, in 1887, the first regular coach service, a procession of mountaineers began arriving. They were all after the honour of being first to topple Mt Cook from its unclimbed status.

Dozens of attempts were made, with some men making repeated trips back to the mountain. In 1894 the "colonials" heard that another prominent English climber, E. A. Fitzgerald, was on his way to New Zealand with a Swiss guide to show how to climb Mt Cook. 'That'll be the day,' said the New Zealanders and on Christmas Day, 1894, Tom Fyfe, George Graham and Jack Clarke stood on the summit of Mt Cook, having pioneered a brand-new route from the Hooker Glacier. Fitzgerald was so hurt that he declined to try the mountain. His Swiss friend, Zurbriggen, was less dainty and went right ahead to make the second ascent of the mountain by himself. It should be recorded that Fitzgerald subsequently made several first ascents with Zurbriggen, including Mounts Tasman, Sefton and Haidinger.

103

Since those days the Southern Alps have become the centre of one of the most active climbing countries in the world. The easy access to Mt Cook National Park means a quick start can be made on the ascents. This is not the place to tell it, but the story of mountaineering here is full of colour and adventure. A young man named Edmund Hillary made the first climb of Mt Cook by the south ridge in 1948. Freda du Faur, the earliest liberated women produced in Australia, was an enchanted and enchanting climbing visitor.

The naming of the Southern Alps peaks is a miniature story in itself. Captain J. L. Stokes, of the Royal Navy survey ship *HMS Acheron*, named the highest peak after the great navigator and this example was followed with the use of navigators' names for other high points – Tasman, Hicks, La Perouse, Jellicoe, Sturdee, Vancouver and Malaspina. Dampier, buccaneer as well as navigator, is represented, but only after a change from the original Mt Hector, bestowed by Haast for James Hector, a fellow-geologist who appears in the Mt Aspiring chapter. Other names commemorate people who are identified with the Southern Alps: Haast himself, Darby (Darby Thompson, Hermitage guide), Brodrick, (T. N. Brodrick, a Government surveyor), Dixon (M. J. Dixon, North Canterbury farmer and climber), Du Faur Peak, Green, Lendenfeld, (Dr R. von Lendenfeld, zoologist and surveyor), and Mannering (G. E. Mannering, pioneer climber from 1883). Other names reflect scientific accomplishment – Darwin, de la Beche, Forbes, Haeckel, Elie de Beaumont, Haidinger, Hochstetter and Petermann.

A few walks can be made from the Mt Cook village area, some of them short and easy, some requiring more effort and either boots or strong shoes. Be sure about the time required for longer walks because in this sharp, clear alpine air, distances are deceptive and what looks close may be several kilometres away. The same factor can make the mountains look smaller than they really are and it is salutary to attempt to walk closer to them. You can drive up to the Ball hut for a close look at the Tasman Glacier and a couple of other low altitude huts are within reach of ordinary visitors.

Otherwise, this is a park for mountaineering and high altitude skiing, although the ski-planes operating from the airfield will lift you up to the high levels of the glaciers and let you make a quick tourist mark on the snow. They will also give you one of the greatest scenic flights in the world, whisking you up, up and over the main divide for a landing on the Westland glaciers, dizzying you with sweeping turns among the mountains, showing them to you in a way which surpasses all other viewpoints. For the rest, you will need all the equipment demanded by serious mountain climbing.

Climbing the ridge of Mt Dixon (3010 m), where wind has planed the snow to a sharp edge, a contrast with the softer, more rounded shapes in the background.

One of the most impressive peaks in the park is that of Mt Sefton (3157 m). This view is from an alpine meadow just a short distance from the park headquarters, showing that there are small-scale pleasures to be enjoyed among the vast dimensions of the mountains. Avalanches are common on Mt Sefton – and often large.

Looking down the 28 km-long Tasman Glacier, with Mt Cook proclaiming its dominance over Mt Haidinger (3066 m) and the pyramid shape of Mt Tasman on the right.

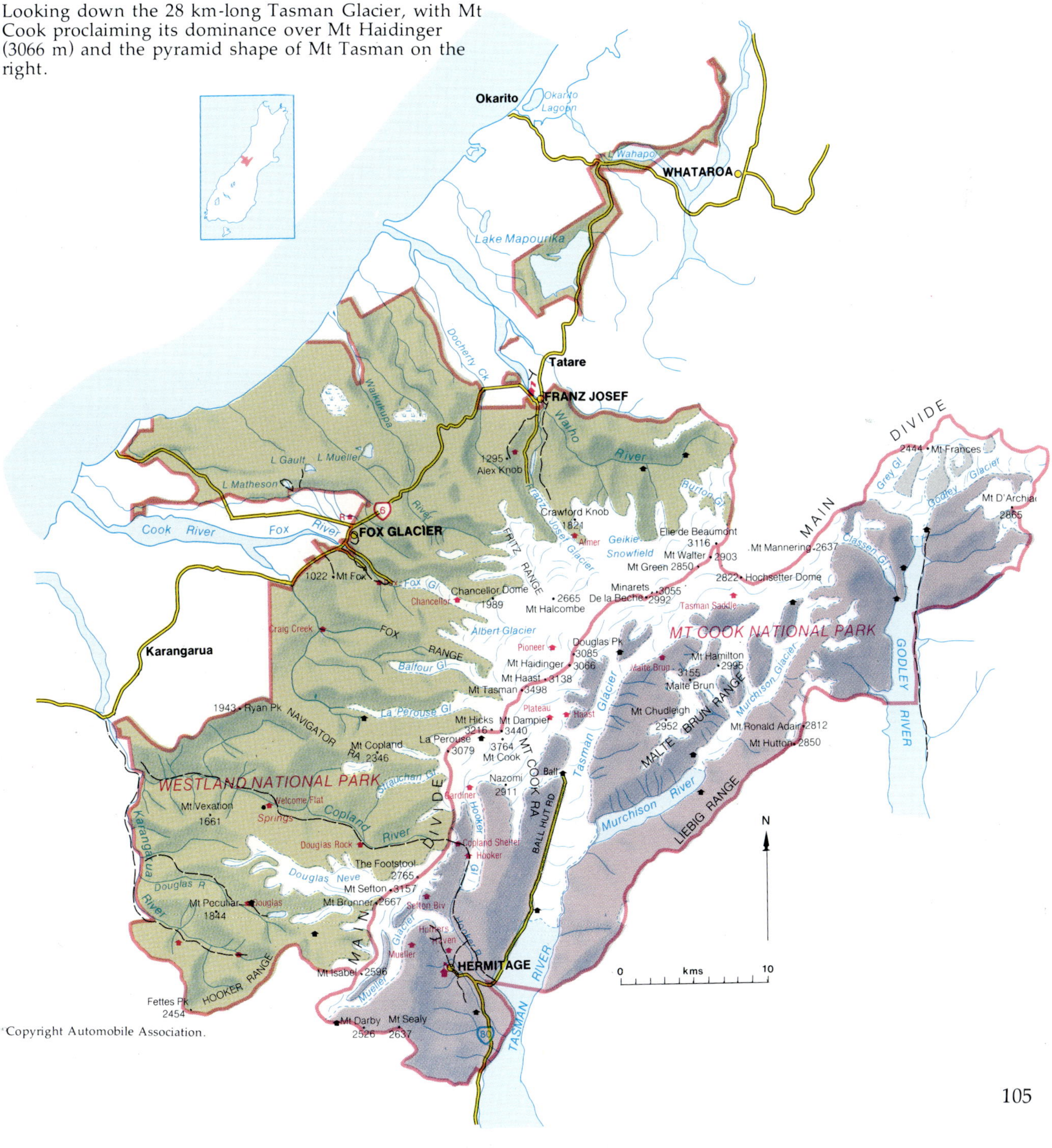

Okarito

Okarito Lagoon

L Wahapo

WHATAROA

Lake Mapourika

Docherty Ck

Tatare

FRANZ JOSEF

Waiho River

Burton Gl

1295 • Alex Knob

Crawford Knob 1824

Almer

Geikie Snowfield

Elie de Beaumont 3116

Mt Walter • 2903

Mt Green 2850

FOX GLACIER

Cook River

Fox River

Waikukupa

L Gault

L Mueller

L Matheson

FRITZ RANGE

Franz Josef Glacier

Minarets • 3055

De la Beche • 2992

2822 • Hochsetter Dome

Tasman Saddle

1022 • Mt Fox

Fox Gl

Chancellor Dome 1989

• 2665

Mt Halcombe

MT COOK NATIONAL PARK

Mt Mannering • 2637

MAIN

DIVIDE

2444 • Mt Frances

Grey Gl

Godley Glacier

Mt D'Archiac 2865

Classen Gl

GODLEY RIVER

Chancellor

FOX RANGE

Albert Glacier

Pioneer •

Douglas Pk • 3085

Mt Hamilton • 2995

Balfour Gl

Craig Creek

Mt Haidinger 3066

Malte Brun • 3155

Murchison Glacier

Karangarua

Mt Haast • 3138

Malte Brun

Mt Tasman • 3498

Plateau

Haast

Mt Chudleigh 2952

MALTE BRUN RANGE

Mt Ronald Adair • 2812

Mt Hutton • 2850

1943 • Ryan Pk

NAVIGATOR

La Perouse Gl

Mt Hicks Mt Dampier 3216 • 3440

La Perouse • 3079

Mt Copland RA 2346

• 3764 Mt Cook

Tasman Glacier

Murchison River

LIEBIG RANGE

WESTLAND NATIONAL PARK

Strauchon Gl

MT COOK RA

Nazomi 2911

MAIN DIVIDE

Mt Vexation 1661

Welcome Flat Springs

Copland River

Hooker Gl

Ball

BALL HUT RD

N

Douglas Rock

The Footstool 2765

Copland Shelter

Hooker

Douglas Neve

Mt Sefton • 3157

Mt Peculiar 1844

Douglas R

Douglas

Mt Bronner • 2667

Sefton Biv

kms

0 10

HOOKER RANGE

Mueller Gl

Mt Isabel 2596

Hooker

Hooker

Mueller

Glacier

HERMITAGE

TASMAN RIVER

Fettes Pk 2454

Mt Darby 2526

Mt Sealy 2637

80

New Zealand skiing used to be centred on Mt Cook National Park. It started in 1893 when three New Zealanders, M. Dixon, G. Mannering and T. Fyfe used native ingenuity to cross the park's Grand Plateau wearing skis made from the blades of a reaper-binder. Orthodox skis were imported and used in 1909. Between the two world wars, skiing was an important winter sport at Mt Cook, the Ball Glacier being used for New Zealand championships. After World War II the demand for longer and steeper courses caused a shift of big events to Coronet Peak and Mt Ruapehu. Mt Cook National Park has snowfields which are immensely bigger than those of the other two skiing centres but the steepness of the Southern Alps makes access to them difficult.

Harry Wigley, of the Mt Cook Tourist Company, now better known for its Mt Cook Airlines operation, showed the way to overcome this problem when he landed a light plane fitted with skis of his own design on the upper Tasman Glacier in 1955. His design allowed the aircraft to use wheels on an airfield and skis in the snow, all on the one flight. Immediately the whole concept of high alpine activity changed. Climbers could be landed well up in the mountains. Ski-mountaineering became more feasible because the plane could save a lot of hard climbing. But for the skiing enthusiasts, the Wigley invention opened up the whole length of the Tasman Glacier. Its 24 km skiable length, for the experienced only, provides perhaps the ultimate ski experience available anywhere on the globe.

Ski planes take skiers to the tops of the glaciers for some of the world's most exhilarating ski runs.

Bird, plant and animal life is not as diverse in this park as in others. But there is still variety and the plant world shows just how adaptable it is to the harsh conditions here. There are more than 400 species of ferns, mosses, herbs, trees, shrubs and grasses, from the tough, spiny matagouri shrub and grotesque wild spaniards with their cruel spikes to lichens growing high up on the summit rocks of Mt Cook. This is the land with which the so-called Mt Cook lily is identified – in fact a giant mountain buttercup whose fame is rightly world-wide.

Even although snow and ice cover two thirds of the park, there is still room for plants. A South Island edelweiss (*Leucogenes grandiceps*) clutches a small piece of territory.

The tip of Mt Cook is reflected in one of the Red Lakes, a group of tarns on the side of Mt Sebastapol. Their name comes from a red weed growing under the water. A 1½ hour walk from Mt Cook village, this area provides superb views of the major peaks and many of the lower ones and allows an appreciation of their relative heights.

The wingless mountain grasshopper lives in large colonies in parts of the park.

The giant mountain buttercup (*Ranunculus lyallii*) the glory of New Zealand's alpine plants. Often called the Mt Cook lily, it is the emblem of the park and of a New Zealand airline which serves this area. Its large, saucer-like leaves may be more than 30 cm in diameter and its flower stems between 60 and 120 cm tall. The flowers are between 5 and 8 cm in diameter. It is a noble plant and the largest and finest ranunculus in the world.

Birds include the New Zealand falcon, an aggressive creature which will attack you if you get too close to its nest, dive-bombing you in a frightening way. The pipit, New Zealand pigeon, yellow-breasted tomtit, South Island fantail, bellbird, grey warbler, morepork, banded dotterel and South Island pied oystercatcher are among the park's other birds.

The real character of the park is the kea, a remarkable bird, surely unique. It is an alpine parrot, but that is a bald description for a bird in which is combined the silliness of a March hare, the cheekiness of a debt-collector, the swagger of a pirate, the curiosity of Sherlock Holmes, the cunning of a bookmaker and the spirit of a clown. What better guide to its whimsical nature than the fact that it likes to skate on its backside down ice-coated corrugated iron roofs?

The kea is an olive green colour, with bright orange flashes under its wings and a sharp hooked beak which is almost clever enough to sew a sail. Bold, quite unafraid of humans, the kea will test your bootlaces for tightness, examine the robustness of windscreen wipers and radio aerials and maybe invite itself to lunch with you. It is a charming, if slightly irresponsible, bird and it is the source and subject of innumerable campfire stories.

Mt Cook National Park ranges mightily across the southern sky. It is to be treated with great respect by those who go among its peaks and icefields. But it repays that respect with the most splendid alpine spectacle it is possible to find anywhere. You can either venture among it, or relax in the warmth of the Hermitage and simply admire from a distance. Here, even that will give you something to remember.

Mt Sefton from Kea Point, at the end of a nature walk from Mt Cook village. From here the blue-green faces, up to 120 m thick, of the hanging glaciers on the mountain can be seen. Frequent avalanches from them make spectacular viewing.

Imagination is required to connect the giant spaniard (*Aciphylla scott-thomsonii*) with the humble carrot, to whose family it belongs. Its needle spikes can cause a painful wound.

A kea casts a calculating and speculative eye over its surroundings.

The everlasting daisy (*Helichrysum bellidioides*) sends up tall flower stems from its creeping mat of leaves.

Mount Aspiring National Park

Take a long tumult of high mountains, clenched here and there by frozen ice plateaus, spread with an icing of glaciers, lashed and beaten by brutal storms rolling in from the Tasman Sea, draw a line around it and call it Mt Aspiring National Park. If that description seems harsh, it does no more than justice to the conditions prevailing along the massed ridges of rock which the Southern Alps thrust up along the length of the park. There is also great beauty of an austere kind.

There are more gentle aspects of the park but it is essentially a mountain wilderness which offers a formidable challenge to people with a high sense of adventure matched by courage, physical fitness and agility and an immunity to cold, drowning and starvation. So the early explorers, surveyors, prospectors and mountaineers found its high regions and the land is unchanged.

The park is the second largest in the network but it defers to no other in the extent of its high mountains. The mountain after which it is named rises to 3036 m and presents one of the most impressive shapes in the skies of New Zealand. It rises sharply along four ridges from its surrounding ice fields and stands well clear of all other mountains in the park, although this is disguised from eastern viewpoints because it is west of the main divide of the Southern Alps. To north and south stretches a great raised table-land of peaks, up to the vigorous Haast River, down to the Humboldt Mountains and the boundary of Fiordland National Park. The Maori had an apt name for it – Titiraurangi, 'Land of Many Peaks Piercing the Clouds.'

To the east are two glaciated lakes of Wanaka and Hawea, to the west the Tasman Sea, all around other mountains, rivers, lakes and forest, all playing scenic court to the dominant mountains of the park.

The massive tooth of Mt Aspiring stands clear of the mountains around it, a forceful symbol of the high plateau of mountains which form the major part of Mt Aspiring National Park. This photograph from Mt Bevan shows the neve of one of the glaciers which surround Mt Aspiring.

R. Struthers

The wild, magnificent roof of the park.

Mt Aspiring is the highest New Zealand mountain outside Mt Cook National Park. It is perhaps the most distinctive shape in the whole Southern Alps chain because of its sharpness and isolation from competitors. From north-east or south-west it is a slender arrowhead, while from east or west its shape is much broader. It carries the largest glaciers of any single mountain other than those in Mt Cook National Park. It is an apt symbol of the park for those who aspire to the high peaks.

It is possible to enjoy relatively easy walking or tramping holidays in the park, especially when summer warms the river flats in the valleys which swoop down out of the mountains. There is good access, too, for those who simply want to drive into the outer fringes of the park for day visits. The Haast highway between the West Coast and Wanaka, which crosses the Southern Alps at Haast Pass, skirts the northern boundary of the park and cuts through its northeast corner before leaving the park to continue down the shore of Lake Wanaka. From the highway you can appreciate something of the park's scale. But it is necessary to be reasonably fit if you are to get to grips with the higher beauties of the park. And to be aware of the hazards of tramping in an alpine region where storms can gather quickly and unleash torrential rain which will rapidly bring up rivers and streams. Temperatures can drop fast. This is not a park for the casual walker.

The park was not created until 1964, which makes it the youngest of our national parks. With an area of some 287,000 ha, it was born of the wish of climbing and tramping clubs to preserve the area from development which could harm its natural character. The thought of development is unlikely to have occurred to those brave and resourceful men who first explored and mapped the area which is now the park. Some of their names spell out the history of the earliest European penetration of the South Island's most remote recesses.

This land was familiar to the earliest Maori although it is likely that the highest and least accessible parts of the park were beyond the capabilities of their clothing. However the Maori travelled far in search of food and greenstone and they knew ways across the Southern Alps – Haast Pass and Harris and Greenstone Saddles for instance. During the moa-hunting period from about 1050 to 1600 the Maori are known to have had a site above Glenorchy near the head of Lake Wakatipu. The first pakeha did not reach the district until 1853, when Nathaniel Chalmers became the first to sight Lake Wakatipu from the Nevis Mountains. In 1857 the Otago Provincial Council's chief surveyor, J. T. Thomson, saw and named Mt Aspiring after climbing Mt Grandview at Hawea.

The Haast Highway reveals at every straight and corner a fresh view of Mt Aspiring National Park, from river to hill to mountain.

The Wilkin River is typical of those which run fast and wide out of the mountains of the park. Beech forest dominates this eastern side of the park, but there are grassy river flats too which give trampers good access to the upper river valleys.

Mighty snow slopes feed the winding Wilkin River, which charts a meandering course down the gravel-filled bed of an old glacier path.

A climber pauses to examine a rock face which will thoroughly test his skills and experience.

The discovery of gold in Otago in 1861 brought a flood of prospectors which washed up as far as the southern part of the park, with strikes in the nearby Arrow and Shotover Rivers. The Otago Provincial Council sent its geologist, James Hector, to explore the area from west of the main divide of the Southern Alps to the coast. In 1863 he went up the Matukituki Valley, that convenient access route into the lower eastern side of the park, crossed the divide at the head of the west branch of the Matukituki and struggled down the Waipawa River to the Arawata River before having to turn back for lack of food.

The first white man to reach the coast from the Otago interior was a miner, P. Q. Caples, who at about this time travelled alone from Lake Wakatipu to Martins Bay, making a very useful map as he went. A few months later Hector completed his journey – from the opposite direction, landing at Martins Bay by boat and travelling up the Hollyford Valley. At the other end of the park, Haast Pass was first crossed in 1863, not by geologist Sir Julius von Haast, but by Charles Cameron. Haast crossed a little later. News of the pass brought the gold seekers and so tough did they find the country that the idea of a road through here seemed impossible.

One of the most arduous explorations in the region of the park area was made by another propector, A. J. Barrington. A conscientious diarist, Barrington left a vivid record of difficult river crossings, terrifying descents of sheer precipices, starvation, snowstorms, bitter cold and rain, rain, rain. Barrington and two companions were the first pakeha to find the Olivine Ice Plateau, at the southwest extremity of the park.

The ice plateau is the highest part of the Olivine Range, which runs northwards out of the park towards the coast of Jackson Bay. It is about 12 km long and up to 3 km wide and is one of the bleakest places in New Zealand. Although not as high as other parts of the park, it exercises over its visitors a baleful influence, arising from its exposure to western storms and from the extreme difficulty of reaching it on foot. Barrington and his party had to get over this barrier to return to Lake Wakatipu after frightful hardships in the valleys, gorges, and bush along the western boundary of the park. It was a climb born of desperation to return to civilisation and the men paid a desperate price, facing the glaciers and snowfields of a scene with nothing but 'mountains of snow as far as we could see, in every direction but west.' Their return journey was made through snow and sleet, with a ghastly time negotiating the Olivine River gorge, hungry and cold, one of their meals, 'the sweetest meat we ever ate,' being a rat. They emerged from the bush barely alive, frost-bitten, the bones of cheeks and noses bared by exposure. It was to be 70 years before men again trod the grim Olivine Ice Plateau.

In 1883 there came on the scene two men who were important to the exploration of the Southern Alps – surveyor and explorer Gerhard Mueller and field surveyor Charles Douglas, the Mr Explorer Douglas who vies with Thomas Brunner for the title of greatest European explorer in New Zealand. They traversed and mapped much of the Westland side of the park area and in 1885 they travelled up the Arawata River, named the Williamson River and the Andy Glacier feeding it, after Andy Williamson, who had visited the Arawata two years before, and climbed Mt Ionia for survey purposes, cutting steps up the ice. Mueller named the Olivine Range after a mineral of that name and also named the series of small tributaries which run into the Waipara River and the mountains of the Haast Range from which they fall. The names reflect his interest in ships. From the coastal paddle steamer Waipara and its crew he took the name of the river and its tributaries – Steward, Fireman, Binnacle, Funnel, Stoker, Rudder, Cook, Third Mate, Second Mate and Bilgewater. His naming of Mounts Corner Post, Moonraker, Stargazer, Mainroyal and Rolling Pin carries a nautical flavour.

Later that year, Douglas went up the Okura River in an attempt to find passes between Westland and Otago and had to be content with finding four which were suitable only for 'an Alpine Explorer or other Lunatic.' In 1891 Mr Explorer Douglas (as he became known from his official reports) went up the Waiototo River, struggling with river and rain, at more than 50 years of age making hard work of humping provisions. His companionable dog Betsey Jane, surely the most travelled New Zealand has ever seen, helped relieve the misery – and gave birth to a pup on the trip. He climbed Mt Ragan (2259 m), the last 600 m in his socks because the rock slabs were too smooth for his boots to grip. He travelled up the Te Naihi River, a tributary of the Waiototo, and climbed high into the mountains, where he came close to death from exposure. Only his fearlessness and hardiness saved him.

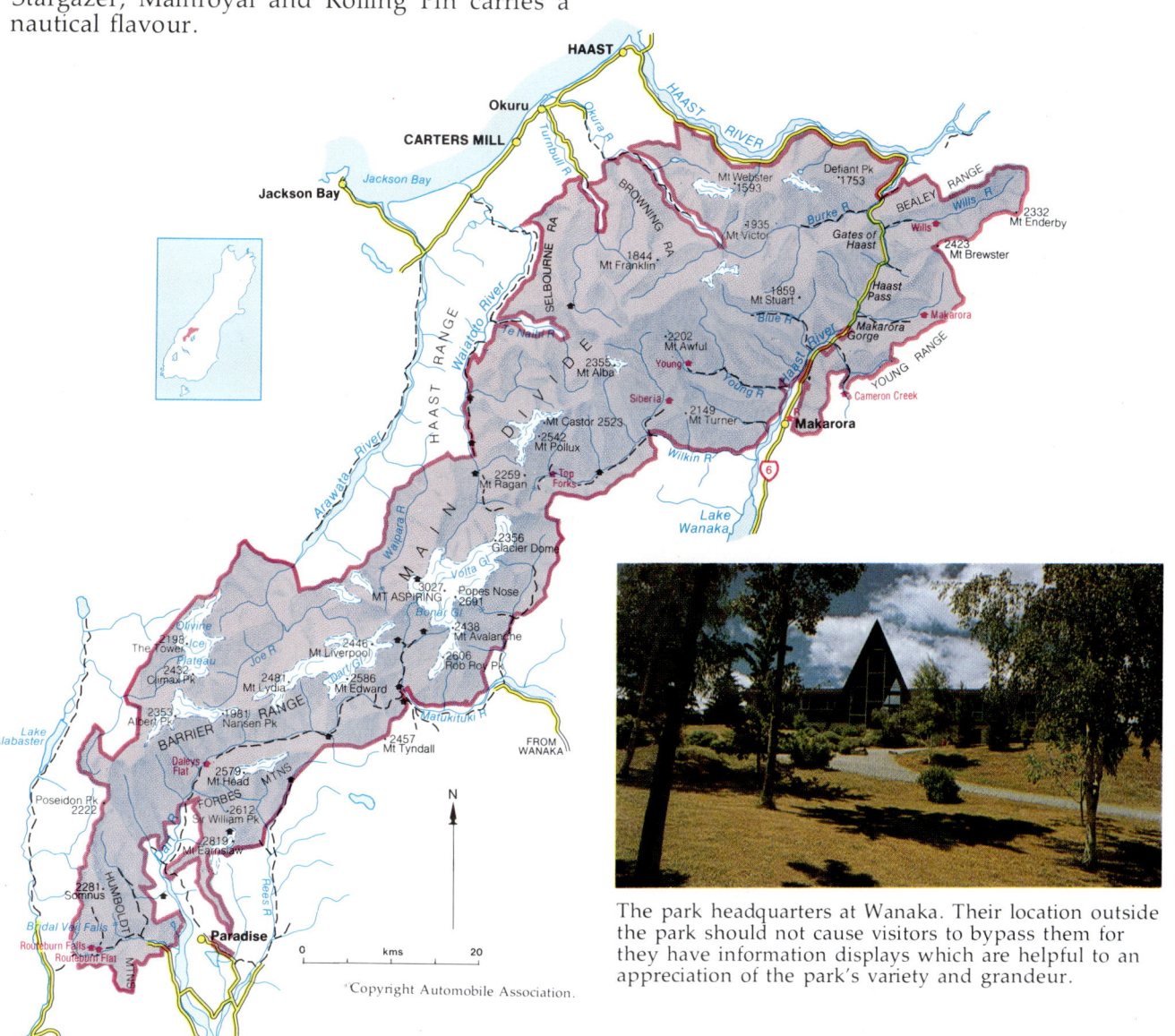

'Copyright Automobile Association.

The park headquarters at Wanaka. Their location outside the park should not cause visitors to bypass them for they have information displays which are helpful to an appreciation of the park's variety and grandeur.

Rainbow Col is cut off from Rainbow Valley by sheer rock walls. Cascades emphasise the vertical dislocation of rock which occurred during mountain-building in the park.

Aspiring National Park

The rigours of climate which mountaineers meet in the Southern Alps are mild compared with the conditions which ruled over the park during the Ice Age, when an ice cap probably covered all but the very highest peaks. The clutch of the ice is well demonstrated by the terminal moraine left at Kingston by the glacier which once flowed 130 km from the Alps down the valley which is now Lake Wakatipu. There are examples in the Haast Pass and Arawata and Cascade Saddles of the way the flowing ice smoothed the rock which once lay beneath the sea before being folded and elevated into mountains. Most of the high peaks are sharp and angular in keeping with the sheerness of Aspiring itself. There are many hollows, or cirques, scooped out by old glaciers, some of them forming hanging valleys which are sometimes filled by lakes, such as Mystery and Unknown.

R. Cobb

For the next 45 years the mountains and valleys of the park were the preserve of Arawata Bill – William O'Leary, a mineral prospector who has been elevated to almost legendary status. He was in fact a patient, tough character who liked the isolation of this country and who was adept at discovering various routes through it. He is commemorated by O'Leary Pass in the Barrier Range and his blazes and cairns were of value to the mountaineers who began rediscovering the southern peaks of the park in the 1930's. One of them was J. T. Holloway, who led climbing parties over three seasons between 1935 and 1938, climbing many peaks in the Barrier Range and exploring the Olivine Ice Plateau in detail, imaginatively naming Mounts Blockade, Intervention, Darkness, Gable, Climax, Destiny, Typhoon and Tempest. He and his companions made many first ascents and in 1937 they met and stayed with Arawata Bill at a hut on the Dart River.

Sunshine warms alpine grassland under the cold shape of Mt Castor. The rock face is sheer and hundreds of metres high, a challenge to climbers who find in this park an infinite variety of conditions.

Rushing river, bounding waterfall and high hills are both reward and warning for people who go high into the park.

Much of the park is a long, broken roof of rock, snow and ice but as it drops down into gorge and valley, its harsh outlines soften into thick forests and grassy river flats which on a fine summer day give the park a benign appearance contrasting with its upper ruggedness.

Beech is the main forest type in the park. Silver beech is the dominant species in the wetter half west of the main alpine divide and commands the topmost level of forest up to the timberline. Mountain beech is found mostly in the southerly section of the park mixed with silver beech in the western valleys. Red beech too is found mainly in the southern section of the park and in the Dart Valley is one of the last great stands of red beech in New Zealand. In the lower Haast Valley, silver birch mingles at lower levels with typical Westland rain forest, while the lower river valleys to the south support rimu, totara, kahikatea, miro and kamahi. Southern rata grows on the western side of the divide.

Sub-alpine scrub near the snowline is typical of the Southern Alps, with snow totara, celery pine, coprosmas, alpine daisies and hebes and the great mountain buttercup. There is also speargrass, which Barrington complained was 'our greatest torment, as its sharp points are like so many needles running into our legs'.

Alpine flowering plants have suffered severe damage by deer, especially in the more inaccessible areas west of the main divide. The plant regime has in many places been significantly altered, plants which are not liked by deer replacing those which are. Tall snow tussock has completely disappeared from some places. Hares have contributed to the change.

Since helicopter deer-hunting began reducing herds in the park, there has been a recovery of bush and alpine plants which can only be described as dramatic. It is quite clear that these national parks cannot continue to be used as a farm for animals hunted for sport; the levels at which deer herds must be maintained to satisfy the hunter's desire to find them is much higher than New Zealand bush can withstand. The danger was forseen in this area in 1922, when it was warned that deer were becoming a menace to the bush, yet there are still those who would argue that a stable deer population is required for hunting purposes.

The Haast Highway gives a view of the park to many more people than could ever be found tramping or climbing in the park because even short forays from the park boundary up into the hills require a sharp weather eye, a basic knowledge of mountain survival and good clothing. The Haast Pass is the lowest pass across the Southern Alps at a height of 562 m and the highway on both sides passes through magnificent mountain, hill, forest, river and lake country.

Late afternoon and time for a restful halt along the Haast Highway.

T. Pitman

Speargrass which grows on the lower grassland of the park is a fierce plant and painful to the unwary tramper. This is *Aciphylla monroi.*

R. Cleland

The Harris Saddle track crosses tussock land between jagged peaks on the Routeburn Track to Fiordland National Park. The saddle (1277 m) is the highest point on the track.

The snow marguerite (*Senecio scorzoneroides*), one of the many species of this plant, grows in the alpine herbfields of the park.

T. Pitman

Swamp musk (*Mazus radicans*).

T. Pitman

The drive through the lower Haast Valley is along a valley floor which was once probably scoured out well below sea level by the glacier which used to flow down it and far out into an iceberg-dotted sea. It had been filled up by rock and gravel eroded off the Southern Alps over thousands of years. The river can flood here to almost a kilometre wide. Thunder Creek Falls pouring into the Haast over a canyon which the river has cut down through the old glacial valley bed, the Gates of Haast, a gorge cut by the water though schist rock, and several river flats, all surrounded by towering mountains, are among the features of this scenic road. A booklet on the Haast Highway published by the Park Board is helpful to an appreciation of the journey.

The Matukituki Valley gives good access to the eastern boundary of the park and in fine weather it is an easy walk from the end of the road to a view of the Rob Roy Glacier. There is access from Queenstown to the southern area of the park for casual visitors. The drive up the side of the immense old glaciated valley of Lake Wakatipu is one of the finest in New Zealand and ends at the broad valleys of the Dart and Rees Rivers. One branch of the the road travels past Diamond Lake to well-named Paradise. Another branch of road travels through beautiful red beech forest to the lower Routeburn Valley 3 km inside the park boundary, where there are picnic and parking facilities. From the end of both roads there are splendid views of the park's mountains. The area is the starting point for the Routeburn Track which joins Mt Aspiring and Fiordland National Parks. It provides a tramp of three or four days and superb views of forest, lake, river and mountains as well as the opportunity to examine plant and bird life close up. It is a venture suitable only for the reasonably fit and care must be taken with the weather, as part of the route lies above the bushline and is extremely exposed. Snow closes the track in winter.

Mt Aspiring National Park offers only its fringes to the casual tourist. Beyond lies an uncompromising land into which only the expert, fit and redoubtable may go. That is well, for there should always be in this country places where wilderness survives to challenge our sense of adventure and test our human capabilities.

D. Kendall

Several generations of beech trees form a green underworld.

A fire and a rest for a climber in a cave which has long served as a refuge for adventurers in the mountains.

Lake Castalia lies high in the Wilkin Valley mountains, its cold green colour at odds with the sky.

120

Fiordland National Park

Mountains and water are the great scenic themes of Fiordland, largest, wildest and most remote refuge of the children of Tane. The mountains run the length of Fiordland and water surrounds them like a liquid necklace – on the west immense fiords sundering the coastline, on the east a string of beautiful lakes. Fiords and lakes stretch their fingers towards each other and sprinkled between them are countless other lakes, tarns and pools reflecting the heights above. Water so much dissects the land that it seems almost in danger of separating into a system of islands – and even of seceding altogether from the South Island.

High waterfalls leap gracefully from towering rock walls, while tumbling rivers and streams flow in more directions than the compass has points. There are high alpine regions with all their characteristic features of glaciers, hanging valleys, ice-carved amphitheatres – and mountain sides plunging from snowline straight down into the sea. Here are the world's highest sea cliffs. New Zealand's most widespread beech forest rises to the snowline, rain forest inhabits the lower valleys and both give sanctuary to two of the world's rarest birds.

A great New Zealand wilderness of mountain and forest exists here mainly as it did before the coming of man. Its preservation as a national park was inevitable and Fiordland defines itself well for the purpose, its inland boundary being neatly marked for most of its length by lakes separating the mountains from the lower land to the east. Fiordland is one of the largest national parks in the world. Its area of more than 1.2 million ha is almost half as large again as the combined areas of all other New Zealand National Parks.

Milford Sound broods under a lowering sky clearing after rain, with the Bowen Falls tumbling down from the highest sea cliffs in the world, their spray raising a pale ghost above the waters of the fiord.

The majesty and beauty of Fiordland.

Lake Marchant mirrors a Fiordland sky. In the background is Caswell Sound, into which the lake drains by the Stillwater River. This is on the tramping route between Caswell Sound and the South West Arm of Lake Te Anau.

Fiordland National Park is the home of Milford Sound and the Milford Track, which was labelled last century as 'The Finest Walk in the World.' It contains the South Island's biggest lake, Te Anau, and New Zealand's deepest, Manapouri. These places are deservedly world famous as tourist destinations yet they are on the fringe of the park and much of the remaining area is little known and in places unexplored. The mountains and the forest have seen to that. And, it must be admitted, rain which does not so much fall as plunge.

Milford Sound is the best known of the New Zealand fiords and it certainly has a vertical dimension which puts it apart from the others. Some of the other fiords are much longer, running up to 32 km inland. The whole length of the park's coastline is made up of cliffs or steep mountain sides rising straight out of the sea, interspersed with the fiords, which could accommodate all of the world's navies and still leave room for sailing.

Although they are called sounds, these are true fiords – arms of the sea penetrating into steep-sided valleys carved out by the ancient glaciers. There are 16 named fiords in the park, many of them with branching arms at their heads so that exploring all of them is a very substantial undertaking. Milford Sound is the northern-most and the labyrinth formed by Chalky and Preservation Inlets and their asscociated sounds are the most southerly coastal indentations.

D. Wakelin

This inundation of the land by long and narrow stretches of water is the classic legacy of the glaciers of the Ice Age. They dug their long furrows deep into the land with such an intense weight of ice that the beds of the main flows went well below sea level. As the ice retreated after the end of the last glaciation about 14,000 years ago, the sea claimed what the glaciers gave up and made the fiords. Inland, the glaciers' burrowings were succeeded by Lakes Te Anau and Manapouri, the arms which they extend deep into the mountains revealing the glaciers' old paths. The glaciers also carved the long, slender shapes of Lakes Monowai, Hauroko and Poteriteri in the southeastern corner of the park.

The depth which the glaciers reached is awesome. Lake Manapouri's surface is 178 m above sea level but it is 447 m deep so that its bed is 269 m below the level of the sea just a few kilometres away. Lake Te Anau is 202 m above sea level but its 396 m depth also places its bed below sea level, a feature shared by Lakes Wakatipu, Wanaka and Hawea, the other great southern lakes of New Zealand.

The glaciers which flowed to the west dug even deeper. Imagine the walls of Milford Sound covered almost to the top by ice, ice which descended so thickly that it kept the sea at bay while doing its work on the bed of the sound. The glaciers in fact excavated Milford Sound to a depth of 396 m and cut its walls so sheer that there is no anchorage within even a metre or so of the shoreline. These walls are the highest sea cliffs in the world, rising about 1.5 km above the waterline and with a total height of almost 2 km.

The sounds of Fiordland are all deep and offer safe haven to the largest ships. So Captain James Cook found in 1773 during his second voyage to New Zealand, when on March 26 he selected Dusky Sound as the base for repairs to his sloop *Resolution*. It was his first landing in this part of New Zealand; he had sailed *Endeavour* around the coast during his first voyage of 1770 but had not been able to effect a landing – it was too late in the day at Dusky Sound, the wind was uncertain at Doubtful Sound. Cook left names but no footprints.

One of the famous sights of New Zealand: Mitre Peak and Milford Sound. The peak is 1692 m high. On the left is Sinbad Gully, a special area for the protection of the kakapo.

Fiordland National Park

Hall Arm of Doubtful Sound is typical of the soaring cliffs which were cut so steeply by glaciers before the sea invaded the valleys to create the fiords.

125

A grass lily *(Herpolirion novae-zelandiae)* which grows in lowland bogs and swamps. It has grass-like leaves and produces a single, large flower.

T. Pitman

N

0   kms   25

Big Bay
Martins Bay
Jamestown
Lake McKerrow
Lake Alabaster
PEMBROKE
Milford Sd **WILDERNESS**
St Anne Pt **AREA**
SINBAD GULLY
SPECIAL AREA
Mitre Pk
1692
1933
Poison Bay
Llawrenny Pks
Doughboy
Sheerdown Pk
Mt Ada
1891
Mt Gifford
Mt Tutoko
2746
Mt Madeline
2537
Mt Talbot 2158
2316
Mt Lyttle
MILFORD SOUND
187
Boatshed Homer
Tunnel
Homer
2332
207
Mt Christina
Hollyford
Dumpling Mt Elliott
2003
Sutherland Falls Crows Nest
Quintin
Mintaro
Castle Mt
2130
Mt Park 2018
Ngatimamoe Pk
2173
Rompolona
Sutherland Sd
Bligh Sd
George Sd
Clinton Forks
Cascade Creek
Glade House
FRANKLIN MOUNTAINS
GLAISNOCK
WILDERNESS AREA
Caswell Sd
Mt McDougall
2036
STUART MOUNTAINS
Eglinton
1859
Mt Donald
1585
Charles Sd
Mt Pisgah
1556
Nancy Sd
North Fiord
Middle Fiord
Te Ana-au
Caves
Te Anau Downs
Thompson Sd
Mt Irene
1879
Dana Pks
1722
LAKE
TE ANAU
Secretary Island
Coronation Pk 1765
MURCHISON MOUNTAINS
SPECIAL
(TAKAHE) AREA
SPECIAL
AREA
Doubtful Sd
Febrero Pt
1570
Mt Maury
South Fiord
Mt Fannin
1570
KEPLER MOUNTAINS
Dagg Sd
Towing Hd
Mt Soaker
1593
TE ANAU
Commander Pk
1274
Mt George
1598
West Arm
Pomona I
LAKE
MANAPOURI
Mt Troup
1518
Mt Wilmot
Black Giants
1640
1544
Mt Crowfoot
1695
MANAPOURI
Breaksea I
Breaksea Sd
1518
Mt Watson
Mt Titiroa
1710
HUNTER MTS
Resolution
Island
Wet Jacket Arm
Greebe R
Five Fingers Pt
Anchor I
Long I
Cooper I
Kathryn Pk
1433
Clarke
Cleughearn Pk
1574
MONOWAI
Dusky Sd
Long Burn
Lake
Monowai
West Cape
Lake
Hauroko
CAMERON MOUNTAINS
Cunaris Sd
Lake
Poteriteri
Long Sd
Cape Providence
Chalky Inlet
Chalky I
CLIFDEN
R
Preservation Inlet
Coal I
Puysegur Pt
L. Hakapoua

©Copyright Automobile Association.

126

On his second journey, the coast seemed kinder and Cook's entry into Dusky Sound, which he named Dusky Bay, introduced the first substantial presence of the pakeha in New Zealand. His ship had been four months at sea and Dusky Sound was a welcome harbour for recuperation. Here he and his crew stayed for 47 days, making history as they went – they killed seals for fresh meat for the first time in New Zealand, made the first ship repair yard, established the first brewery using rimu and manuka, made the first tea, from manuka leaves, shot the first Fiordland birds, introduced the local Maori to the musket and were themselves introduced unwillingly to the infamous Fiordland sandfly.

Cook's stay at Dusky Sound began the earliest history of pakeha residence in New Zealand. By the end of the 18th Century, the sounds of Fiordland had seen more Europeans than the whole of the rest of New Zealand. But for 18 years after Cook sailed away, Fiordland was left to the sparse Maori population. In 1791 Captain George Vancouver, who had been a lieutenant under Cook on the *Resolution*, brought the *Discovery* into Dusky Sound, in the company of Captain Broughton in the *Chatham*. They left their names in the Vancouver and Broughton Arms of Breaksea Sound.

Sealing and whaling were the first European industries in New Zealand and Fiordland was their early base. In 1792 John Leith and 12 men landed from the *Britannia* to hunt the New Zealand fur seal, *Arctocephalus forsteri*, the only one which breeds on the New Zealand mainland and which is now fully protected. During their year's stay, they began building a ship in case the *Britannia* should fail to return. However the *Britannia* turned up and took off the party and 4500 skins. The ship was completed by the crew of the *Endeavour*, a merchant ship which arrived and was run aground to become New Zealand's first shipwreck. The crew finished the sealers' partly-built ship and launched her as the *Providence*, the first ship built in New Zealand or Australia from native timber.

Regular sealing in Fiordland continued into the 19th Century. A Captain Grono had a sealing base in Doubtful Sound until 1823 and it is thought that he discovered and named Milford Sound after Milford Haven in Wales, the country of his birth. He named Bligh Sound after the famous Captain of the *Bounty*. Grono's own name is given to Mt Grono and Grono Bay on Secretary Island. Elizabeth Island, near the head of the sound, takes its name from Grono's wife. Another sealer's name has gone to Dagg Sound.

Sealers, and after them the whalers, hunted their quarry almost out of existence in the local waters and by about the mid-19th Century both groups of hunters were gone from these shores. From 1848 to 1851, HMS *Acheron*, a paddle steamer, carried out its great survey of the New Zealand coast for the British Admiralty. The survey was rewarding: Milford Sound was described as one of the grandest sights in the southern hemisphere; the ships's surgeon, Lyall, was also a botanist and he gathered an extensive collection of plants, discovered the largest and most beautiful buttercup in the world, *Ranunculus lyallii*, the so-called Mt Cook lily, and caught kakapo, the flightless ground parrot, which made a stir in the scientific world and which is now rare.

Acheron Passage, between Breaksea and Dusky Sounds, marks the survey ship's visit. As sealers, whalers and surveyors moved out, the first settlers began moving in. One of the first at Milford Sound was Donald Sutherland, who in 1880 discovered Sutherland Falls and in 1883 Sutherland Sound while sailing down the coast. Explorers pushed west from the lakes but their journeys were tentative. So precipitous was the land and so impenetrable the bush on the west of the ranges that few people cared to try inland exploration from the sounds. In 1897 E. H. Wilmot found a way across Wilmot Pass between the West Arm of Lake Manapouri and Deep Cove at the head of Doubtful Sound. A tourist track was cut over the route, which is generally followed by today's road. Wilmot also found a route from Lake Manapouri along the Spey and Seaforth Rivers to the head of Dusky Sound. Today it is a tramping route.

New Zealand fur seals, the only kind which breeds on the New Zealand mainland, sunbathing on a favourite rock.

Meanwhile, the sea provided the only practicable way of reaching the fiords. Quintin McKinnon, who was important to the opening up of Fiordland, had travelled with S. Tucker from the South West Arm of Lake Manapouri's Middle Fiord to Caswell Sound in 1887. Richard Henry, another notable Fiordlander, who from 1894 to 1909 was the naturalist caretaker of Resolution Island, had reached George Sound from the North West Arm of the lake in 1889. But the real challenge was to discover an overland tourist route to Milford Sound. McKinnon succeeded with E. Mitchell by finding McKinnon Pass in 1888. A track was subsequently cut for the famous walk, on which McKinnon Pass is the highest point. 'The Finest Walk in the World' became the subject of tourist advertisements and its path has remained unchanged since then.

With the Milford Track route established, attention turned to a road into Milford Sound. As with the track, the difficulty lay in finding a practical route through the high and steep mountains which are the conspicuous feature of the northern part of Fiordland National Park. Here the Darran, Wick and Franklin Mountains mark the southern end of the Alpine Fault's influence on the South Island landscape. The fault runs out into the sea near Milford Sound and the mountains to the south become less high, although they are still impressive and extremely rugged peaks in a wild setting.

The park's northern mountains demonstrate in perhaps more dramatic fashion than anywhere else in the South Island, the canyon country formed by very deep glaciers. Both the Milford Track and Te Anau-Milford Road pass between the nearly-vertical mountain walls which are also the dominant aspect of the fiords. This steepness was a problem for road engineers. In 1889 W. H. Homer and G. Barber explored the headwaters of the Hollyford River and discovered the Homer Saddle across the divide which separates the Hollyford and Cleddau Rivers, the latter running into the head of Milford Sound.

The valleys of these two rivers seemed to offer the only route for a road to Milford but the steepness of the mountain walls on both sides of the divide – the ridge of the Homer Saddle is razorbacked – was a difficult barrier. Homer proposed a tunnel which Wilmot, following up Homer's exploration, thought impracticable. Homer persisted: 'No timber wanted, no climbing over ice and snow; no repairs and open all the year round. The size of tunnel 7ft 6in high by 6ft wide, at say £1.15. a foot – $2100. This should open a good horse track all through . . . These are facts, and a party can be found to accept the work at the figures tomorrow – and glad of the chance.' Homer was supported by a Public Works Department report in 1890 but the cost was considered excessive. The Great Depression of the 1930s provided the impetus and by 1934 the road

from Te Anau had reached the eastern side of the divide.

Work on the tunnel began in July, 1935. It was a formidable task. The tunnel is at an altitude of 923 m at the Hollyford Valley portal and 795 m at the Cleddau Valley portal. The mountains around soar to more than 2000 m and rainfall is, in thorough Fiordland and West Coast tradition, about 6000 mm a year. There is danger up here of rock and snow avalanches, and the big scree slopes of the area, plainly seen from the road, caused trouble. Avalanches killed and injured several workers during construction. One in 1937 caused the full 7.3 m diameter tunnel, then one third complete, to be reduced to a smaller drive, which holed through in February 1940. Some enlarging work followed but in 1942 the job closed

R. Cobb

Lake Ada and the Arthur River valley, at the head of Milford Sound, from Barren Peak. Ice once rose almost to the mountain tops and formed the classic U-shape of glaciated valleys. The Milford Track passes along the right hand side of the valley.

From Lake Quill, nestling in a basin high up in the mountains, the Sutherland Falls drop 580 m into Arthur Valley, through which the Milford Track passes. The falls are the highest in New Zealand and among the highest on earth.

for the duration of the war. It was renewed in 1951 and the tunnel opened in 1953. As with all construction projects through the Southern Alps, the road and tunnel is a fine piece of engineering and has opened up to all one of the superb scenic areas of the world.

Few places can offer two such different but equally attractive ways of reaching a beautiful destination as Fiordland does with Milford Sound. The Milford Track usually takes four days to walk, the Milford Road just a few hours to drive. Both offer magnificent views but of course the track removes you from the 20th Century and puts you back on a pioneer trail; the huts along the way are the only concessions to modern convenience. The track can be walked by independent parties using Park Board huts, but the majority join the Tourist Hotel Corporation's guided parties, which get a better class of accommodation. The track involves some hard climbing – McKinnon Pass is 1154 m above sea level – and is not for the frail. Only people with some experience of New Zealand bush tramping should attempt it by themselves, as the weather can be wet and cold at any time. You must book in either case.

The track is walked only in the direction of Milford Sound and starts from the northern end of Lake Te Anau. The first day is spent walking through the incredibly sheer-sided Clinton Canyon, through which the Clinton River flows from its source near McKinnon Pass to Lake Te Anau. The canyon, with its flat floor and steep walls forming a U-shape, is a perfect example of a glaciated valley. The walk along the canyon floor beside the Clinton River passes through beautiful native forest and the whole day is a stirring introduction to the large scale of Fiordland.

The second day takes you over McKinnon Pass, which involves a stiff, zigzag climb and a long descent. There is a monument to McKinnon at the pass, from which there are tremendous views of both the Arthur River, which flows through a steep valley into the head of Milford Sound, and back into Clinton Canyon. This is one of the scenic highlights of Fiordland National Park. Around are several high peaks and on a fine day you obtain a sense of looking out over a primeval and remote landscape.

Members of guided parties may spend the third day visiting Sutherland Falls or walking up other side tracks. The falls spill 580 m from Lake Quill, named after the first man to climb the face at the falls and see the lake, which lies in a basin high up between Mounts Hart and Mackenzie and Couloir Peak. The final day's walk covers the 20 km track down the Arthur River valley, with its bush-covered lower slopes, and passes Lakes Brown and Ada and a number of high waterfalls. The track ends at Sandfly Point, where you will be greeted by New Zealand's most maddening insect. A launch trip across the sound to the Milford Hotel adds a final viewing dimension to a memorable journey.

Moss-laden rain forest on the Milford Track.

Clinton Canyon demonstrates the aptness of its name. It stretches from the northern tip of Lake Te Anau to McKinnon Pass, from where this photograph was taken, the highest point on the Milford Track. Ice once filled this valley on its slow journey from here down to the lake.

G. Gentles

Descending McKinnon Pass into the Arthur River valley on the Milford Track.

G. Gentles

The road to Milford Sound passes through a mountainous landscape which in dimensions is fully the equal of that which Milford Track traverses. Motorists should allow plenty of time for leisurely travel along the road and a day each way is not too much, for there are splendid viewpoints at frequent intervals and opportunities to explore tracks off the road, some of them taking you to lookouts which are not surpassed in the southern hemisphere. And a side trip down the Hollyford River valley road deserves attention.

For 28 km the road follows the shore of Lake Te Anau, giving views of both the South and Middle Fiords before swinging away to follow the Eglinton River up its valley. Here the road introduces you to the peaks of the northern part of the park as it runs between two mountain spurs which include Mt Eglinton (1859 m). The road passes through bush and by lakes, climbing gradually all the way to the source of the Eglinton at the 531 m divide which separates it from the Hollyford River. The gradual climb includes a straight stretch called the Avenue of the Disappearing Mountain because it produces an optical illusion in which a nearby peak appears to sink below the horizon.

At the divide you should, if the weather is satisfactory, allow sufficient time to take the track from the road up to Key Summit. It is suitable for shoes and the climb takes about one and-a-half hours. It is well worth it, for no other place so easily reached from the Milford road provides such a grand view. There is a plane table and an enormous, panoramic view, some of the main points being Mt Christina, Lake Marian, Lake Howden, the Hollyford valley and row after row of mountain top ridges. It is a good place to see the plant community which exists on the alpine moorlands of the park.

Past the divide, the road drops steeply down to the floor of the Hollyford River Canyon. At this point there is another one and-a-half hour walk from the road along a well-formed track to Lake Marian. In the upper Hollyford valley the Milford road lies at the feet of some of Fiordland's highest mountains – Crosscut, (2316 m) Christina, (2502 m) Talbot (2225 m), Students Peak and Mt Suter. Any newcomer to this place will marvel at the way in which the mountains on the northern side of the road rise so steeply from the valley floor.

Under the dominating bulk of Mt Talbot, one of the loveliest shapes in the New Zealand sky, the road plunges into the 1240 m long Homer Tunnel. Before you do so you could try the climb to the Homer Saddle, a steep effort of about an hour, or another track to the Gertrude Saddle.

Beech forest climbs up mountainsides which dwarf campers in the Cascade Creek motor camp operated by the Fiordland National Park Board in the upper Eglinton Valley, on the Milford Road. The camp is a good base for those wanting to take plenty of time to drive to Milford Sound and back.

This is a tougher climb of about two hours and some climbing experience is advisable, at least for one member of the party. The reward of making the climb is an extraordinary view down the upper valley of Milford Sound to the sound itself and of the Darran Mountains, among which are Fiordland's two highest mountains, Tutoko (2746 m) and Madeleine (2537 m). The Darran Mountains are the rough-hewn roof of the park, their granite and diorite rock forming steep and naked walls and this view shows the way in which the sea has invaded the lower reach of the ancient river of ice which cut this landscape so deeply.

On this side of the tunnel the valley head consists of a semi-circle of mountain walls, typical of the scouring action at the head of a glacier formed by ice from side valleys. Glacier ice once rose almost to the top of the mountains ranging down the Hollyford valley here, up to 1000 m above the road level. If you can imagine that you will more clearly see the effects of the glaciers on the mountain sides.

When you enter the tunnel you leave behind the source of the Hollyford. When you emerge you are above the source of the Cleddau River, which the road follows down to Milford Sound, having passed through the divide between them. From the tunnel there is a splendid view of the Cleddau far below, winding with the road down the path of another old glacier. Nature walks at both tunnel portals introduce you to alpine plants which are well worth taking time to see.

The road drops 1000 m from the tunnel to the sound in 17 km, passing on the way the Chasm, for which you must stop, irrespective of your timetable or the weather, to see the Cleddau roaring down into a deep cavern. Just below this point, road travellers get their view of Mts Tutoko and Underwood (2346 m). Finally comes the great sound which is one of the scenic wonders of the world. Nothing could be more appropriate as the finishing point of either a walk or a drive which are themselves of compelling beauty. You can gauge the height of the sound's cliffs by the Bowen and Stirling Falls, which are both more than 150 m high but dwarfed by the rock walls all around. A launch trip is the best way to see the splendour of the sound but there are also walks from the hotel to the Bowen Falls and other viewpoints. Try the Lookout Track for a wide perspective of the sound.

This is the place which calls every visitor to Fiordland National Park, but there is no practical end to the other opportunities for exploring the park. There are, for instance, the other sounds. One of the loveliest is George Sound, which forms part of the boundary of the Glaisnock Wilderness Area, and can be reached by track from the North West Arm of Lake Te Anau's Middle Fiord, using a boat to cross Lake Hankinson at the head of the arm. The sound has steep, forest-covered walls rising to 1500 m in places and a

National Publicity Studios

The kiwi is New Zealand's most famous bird and known throughout the world for its flightless characteristics and long beak, with nostrils at the tip to smell out its insect and grub diet. The brown kiwi is found in National Parks in both islands, there being slight differences between the North Island (*Apteryx australis mantelli*) and South Island (*australis*) sub-species.

Near the Homer Tunnel on the Milford Road, alpine fields show bright colours in contrast to drifting cloud and mountain walls. Boulders at the bottom of a scree slope indicate the mountains' everlasting battle with erosion.

graceful waterfall from Lake Alice at the head of the sound. There is a developed track between the West Arm of Lake Manapouri and Dusky Sound, which can also be reached by a track of similar standard from the head of Lake Hauroko. Neither should be attempted without good equipment and fitness. Sutherland Sound can be reached from the Milford Track in the Arthur River Valley via Staircase Creek and Light River.

There are other overland routes to the sounds, none of them making light travel, and *Moir's Guide Book* (southern section), studied in conjunction with Park Board pamphlets, is indispensable to the serious tramper who is interested in any of them. It is impossible here to describe all of the tramping routes available in this largest of New Zealand wilderness areas and, indeed, most are for the enthusiast. *Moir's Guide Book* is highly recommended for a comprehensive and detailed description of what can be done. It should be mentioned that the Milford road has opened up a great variety of tramping routes in the northern part of the park, especially in the Hollyford-Eglinton area, which includes the southern end of the Routeburn Track into Mt Aspiring National Park.

The lakes of Fiordland are themselves a prime visitor attraction. The bush and the mountains flanking them provide a wonderful backdrop in winter or summer and contribute to the lakes' many different humours. Lake Te Anau is second in area only to Taupo, spreading over 341 square kilometres, and is 65 km long. Its western shoreline, with fiords cutting deep into the mountains, is rugged and forested. On this shore, not far from Te Anau township, are the Te Ana-au Caves, which were rediscovered only in 1948. The name of the lake is derived from the caves, whose name means Cave of Rushing Waters and puzzlement about the origin of the name led to the 1948 finding. These limestone caves are still being formed by the water rushing through them and its formations, waterfalls and glow-worm grotto are one of the highlights of a South Island tour. The caves are lighted and provided with stairs and walkways but retain their natural wonder.

You can take a number of launch trips on the lake and even if you are not walking the Milford Track, a boat journey up the lake to Glade House at the start of the track is one of the most attractive in New Zealand. Your arrival at Glade House may persuade you that you should find time to walk on to Milford. In the other direction, a jet boat ride down the twisting Waiau River is an exciting way of travelling from Lake Te Anau to Lake Manapouri. This is claimed by some to be New Zealand's most beautiful lake and is the second largest in the park. Its original name was Moturau, meaning Many Islands, and Manapouri is short for Manawa-Popore, meaning Anxious Heart, the condition experienced by a traveller in a canoe during a storm.

Manapouri is certainly one of the gems of New Zealand's mountain scenery. It retains an appearance of unaffected charm with its heavily-wooded and curving shores and the mountains rising beyond. It is little wonder that Manapouri has become synonymous with the fight by the conservation movement to preserve from exploitation the remaining natural landscape of what was originally one of the most attractively endowed countries on earth. The Save Manapouri Campaign was a watershed in New Zealand's national conscience on the need to protect this endowment. The heart of the matter is the Manapouri power scheme, which uses water from the lake to drive hydro-electric turbines before discharging it through a tunnel almost 10 km long into Deep Cove in Doubtful Sound. The scheme uses the 180 m difference between the levels of lake and sound to harness water energy to the turbines.

The scheme was already under construction before a national argument developed over the proposal to raise the lake level to increase generating capacity. This would undoubtedly have ruined the lovely shoreline of the lake, as the shoreline of Lake Monowai was spoiled by the raising of its level for a power station built in 1920. The Government of the day desisted from its Manapouri proposal only after a long campaign of pressure from opposing, allied interests. The issue raised serious questions about the inviolability of New Zealand's national parks and the effectiveness of their protective Act of Parliament. Those questions remain.

Ironically, the power scheme without the raised lake level has become a significant tourist attraction in Fiordland National Park. There is no denying that it is an impressive achievement, with its power house hollowed out of solid rock more than 200 m underground. Launches make trips to the lake's West Arm so that visitors can see the powerhouse and then travel over the Wilmot Pass by road to Deep Cove. It is a spectacular drive.

Several local walks around Te Anau township and Manapouri village give the tramper or the casual walker a number of opportunities to look nature in the eye. They are useful for the short-stay visitor. The climb up to Mt Luxmore is not too arduous in summer and presents a fine view of lake and mountain.

National Publicity Studios

North Fiord, Lake Te Anau, with the Stuart Mountains to the left and the Franklin Mountains on the right.

A perfect summer's day on Lake Manapouri justifies the description of the 'loveliest lake in New Zealand.' The Kepler Mountains stand above the Beehive rising from the far shore. This is the view from the Monument, a rock knob 288 m above the lake's Hope Arm.

The main southern lakes of the park should not be forgotten. Although Monowai has its foreshore scarred by ugly tree stumps left by the rise in lake level, it still conveys much sense of attractive wilderness. There is road access to the foot of the lake and a track to Rodger Inlet. Other tracks give access to the appealing tussock high country around Green Lake, another of the small beauties which Fiordland springs upon you, and Island Lake. Lake Hauroko, also with road access, is 37 km long, slender and exquisite. Within it, Mary Island has a 350-year-old Maori burial plot. Lake Poteriteri is less easily accessible overland but also has great charm and good fishing. Only 28 m above sea level and eight kilometres from the coast, rainbow and brown trout have introduced themselves to it. In the very north of the park, Lakes McKerrow and Alabaster add to the splendid variety of waters which this park encloses.

Although Fiordland is rugged and in many places remote, special areas have been set aside to minimise impacts on its natural environment. Introduced animals are the danger. Secretary Island, at the mouth of Doubtful Sound, is classified as a special area to protect its forest and subalpine scrub and grassland from the vandal opossum. The island has an unusual scrub of yellow silver-pine and manuka growing on granite slopes.

Special protection for two rare native birds is the function of other special park areas. The Murchison Mountains have been declared a special takahe area to which entry is by permit only and usually restricted to scientific parties. The takahe is one of the world's rarest birds, a flightless rail, *Notornis mantelli*, which was for 50 years thought to be extinct; it is still perilously close to extinction. Rediscovered by Dr G. B. Orbell in the Murchison Mountains in 1948 during a search for old Maori village sites, the takahe feeds mainly on various plants of the alpine grasslands, which deer have seriously depleted. Another very rare bird confined to Fiordland is the kakapo, the flightless parrot which Lyall discovered. The Pembroke wilderness and Sinbad Gully special areas have been established to protect the habitat of this bird.

The very size of the park poses a considerable problem in the control of eradication of introduced animal pests. Helicopter hunting has helped to bring down deer numbers in recent years, with a consequent improvement in forest cover, but the opossum plague is less easily handled. Stoats are a danger to native birds and are widely distributed. They may be a significant factor in the decline of the takahe and kakapo populations. It says much for the wild nature of the park that despite the worst efforts of deer, chamois, goats, stoats and opossums, it is still possible to see in Fiordland National Park a land much as Cook saw it when he landed at Dusky Sound.

Of all New Zealand's fine array of national parks, Fiordland is the grandest. Mt Cook has the highest and most noble mountains. Westland has the world's most unusual glaciers. Tongariro has the smoking drama of a volcanic past. Egmont thrusts a beautiful cone above green, folded Taranaki in telling contrast. Urewera rolls its forest over hills where Tane's influence may still be felt. Abel Tasman looks out over golden sands fringing beautiful bays. Mt Aspiring raises a long and wild jumble of peaks against the sky. Nelson Lakes lays long waters between mountain reaches. Arthurs Pass humbles man's stretch across the Southern Alps. But wild, remote Fiordland most clearly utters in its fiords, mountains, lakes and forest the strange call which tells those who listen that we too are nature.

The takahe *(Notornis mantelli)*, dramatically rediscovered in 1948 after its extinction had been assumed. It now survives only on the Murchison Mountains west of Lake Te Anau, where alpine plants provide its food.

Another of New Zealand's unusual and, unfortunately, rare birds is the kakapo, which is now found only around Milford Sound in Fiordland National Park. It is a parrot with the facial discs of an owl and has often been referred to as an owl parrot. The bird nests in holes among tree roots and lives mainly on the ground, using well-defined trails through the bush. Although it has quite large and strong wings its flying abilities are strictly limited – about those of a parachute. The kakapo generally feeds at night.

G. Moon

Maritime Parks

New Zealand has one of the most divergent and attractive coastlines in the world, from the fiords and sounds of the South Island to the gentle, sheltered bays which abound along the eastern edge of the land. The coastline with all its delights has made a day at the beach one of New Zealand's most popular summer pleasures.

The coast and its offshore islands provide an environment which has also helped to make yachting and boating a favourite New Zealand pastime. New Zealand has established maritime parks to protect and enhance for public use the foreshores and islands of two areas which are popular for maritime recreation.

The demand for recreational access to beach and bay has been highest in the Auckland region, where more than one quarter of New Zealanders live. It was in the Hauraki Gulf, Auckland's marine threshold, that maritime parks had their genesis. This wide bay encompasses a remarkable variety of harbours, bays and estuaries, islands, reefs and rocks. The invitation of its waterways has stimulated in Auckland a pleasure boat fleet which is the largest in the country and one of the world's biggest in relation to population.

In the 1960s, the growth of Auckland was increasing recreational pressure on the gulf and bringing to both coastal land and offshore islands subdivision and other development. In response to this, the Auckland Regional Authority was establishing on the mainland a network of regional parks with strong orientation towards the bays and beaches of the gulf. This created a climate for similar action to protect the gulf islands from exploitation and preserve traditional public rights to land on them. The result was the Hauraki Gulf Maritime Park, formed in 1967 from public reserves on various islands and since extended by purchase and gift.

The Hauraki Gulf lacks any strict seaward definition but it can conveniently be considered to lie between Tokatu Point in the north and Cape Colville, the tip of the Coromandel Peninsula, in the south. The Hauraki Gulf Maritime Park extends well beyond that natural definition, to Whangaruru North Head near the Bay of Islands and down to the Aldermen Islands off the Coromandel coast. Within the gulf proper, the park's main islands include Rangitoto, Motutapu, Motuihe and Motukorea (Browns Island) as well as part of Rakino and Kawau Islands. Outer islands include Little Barrier, part of Great Barrier, the Mercury Islands except Great Mercury, the Hen and Chickens and Poor Knights.

Rangitoto Island is one of Auckland's symbols, being a perfect example of a volcanic cone and supporting on its lava and scoria slopes a surprising 200 species of ferns and other plants. Motukorea is also a volcanic cone. Several of the inner islands have significant archaeological features from early Maori occupation.

The islands of the park provide breeding grounds and habitats for many birds, including migratory species of seabirds, and in some cases a safe place for rare native birds and other creatures which no longer live on the mainland. Permits are needed to land on some islands. The stitchbird now lives only on Little Barrier Island, known to the Maori as Hauturu (Resting Place of the Wind) because of its regular cloud cap. This island has one of the few large remaining areas of unbrowsed native forest. Kawau Island was once the home of Governor Sir George Grey and his Mansion House and surrounding grounds are within Maritime Park land.

The Marlborough Sounds Maritime Park is composed of more than 100 separate reserves scattered among the lovely inlets and hills of an extensive drowned river system. Established in 1973, it spreads over an area of 29,000 ha in one of New Zealand's most entrancing scenic areas. The labyrinth of land and sea plays host to some of the finest cruising or sailing exploration it is possible to find. Queen Charlotte Sound was a preferred anchorage for Captain Cook. Here in Ship Cove he careened his ship *Endeavour* on his first voyage to New Zealand in 1769, raising the British flag on Motuara, or Island in the Path (of the canoe). He returned here on each of his two subsequent voyages, growing potatoes for the first time in New Zealand and liberating pigs and goats. He was followed by whalers, who had stations at Port Underwood and Te Awaiti.

Settlers fired the forest which once covered the high hills of the sounds and in places burned it over and over again so that regeneration is almost beyond possibility. Elsewhere in the park's reserves, though, the forest is regenerating, bringing back beech, rimu, totara, kohekohe and other plants. As in the Hauraki Gulf Maritime Park, several islands of this park are the exclusive homes of rare birds like the King shag and South Island saddleback.

Not a lizard but a reptile, the tuatara *(Sphenodon punctatus)* is the only survivor of a species which otherwise died out more than 60 million years ago. This distinction has earned the tuatara the name of 'living fossil.' It shares burrows with petrels and shearwaters on several islands of Hauraki Gulf Maritime Park. Taking 50 years or so to grow to full size, the tuatara may reach a length of 300 mm excluding the tail and its lifespan is estimated at about 300 years.

Rangers of the Parks

The glories of New Zealand's National Parks are manifold but speechless. The rangers of the parks are their interpreters.

Rangers articulate the appeal of the parks, helping visitors to understand and connect for themselves the thousands of strands which go to make up the web of life in New Zealand's forests, streams, lakes and mountains. They open the eyes, ears and minds of tens of thousands of yearly visitors to more complete understanding of the precious natural resources which the parks contain. Young New Zealanders in particular have no more important teachers than the rangers of National Parks.

One of the great benefits of the National Parks is that they allow you simply to be aware of nature in a state subject to little or no interference by man. Yet beyond simple awareness are fascinating processes which nature conducts in maintaining a balance between life and death. Rangers help to show you nature without interfering too much with it – on a nature trail, over a billy of tea, in a lecture room, with a film or slide show, in a pamphlet. To understand the importance of National Parks you have to understand the nature of life itself and that is a never-ending quest in which most of us will need some assistance. Park rangers help to provide it.

Rangers are not simply guides, but help to manage the parks. They need to be outdoors people, to have a keen interest in natural history and to like dealing with and helping other people. They must be fit and have a good standard of education, practical abilities including the use of tools, a liking for irregular hours and a cool head for search and rescue hazards.

Rangers' outdoor work includes installing and maintaining tracks, among which are the boardwalks put through sensitive areas like alpine bogs, bridges, huts, picnic areas, campsites, signs, toilets, jetties and boatramps. They organise and prepare displays, give talks and show slides, lead natural history groups and protect the parks from the enemies of unthinking man and alien animals.

The information which rangers disseminate covers many fields: a talk on early Maori occupation of a park area, water and boating safety, the Milford Track, local weather patterns, photographing birds, the environment of the forest; taking a holiday party on a tramping trip and explaining natural features on the way.

The first New Zealand ranger (although that title was not then used) was Richard Henry of Resolution Island, in Dusky Sound. Driven from his Marlborough farm by rabbits, he had moved to Te Anau and become widely known for his exploring bent, great interest in natural history and deep love for native birds. He was chosen as curator and caretaker of Resolution Island when in 1894 it became New Zealand's first bird sanctuary, a result of the effects which even then introduced predators were having on birds on the mainland. Henry became responsible for transferring endangered birds like the kakapo, kiwi and weka. He shifted some 700 birds but in 1900 his dreams were shattered when he discovered a weasel on the island. A true enthusiast for his cause, he was a meticulous recordist of land, weather, fauna and flora. His spirit lives on among the rangers of today.

In 1897 the first caretaker on Little Barrier Island was appointed and the first official park ranger was Alf Cowling, who in 1923 was appointed ranger at Tongariro National Park.

Park rangers are in a rather remarkable position. While acting directly for their fellows, their underlying loyalty is in the end due not to mankind but to the land, the trees, the birds, the animals and all other living things which they protect. They enjoy a very special privilege.

Brewing up for lunch on a nature programme field trip conducted by park rangers at Lake Manapouri.

A ranger at Tongariro National Park talks to members of a school party about a black-backed gull's nest on the shore of the lower Tama Lake.

A natural history lesson for visitors to Fox Glacier lies in the ice which a ranger has plucked from the Fox Glacier immediately below the terminal face of the glacier in the background. Pieces of ice dropping from the face may be much larger than this.

Maritime craft play a useful role for rangers in a park with almost half of its boundary formed by the sea. A ranger lands a marker for a walking route.

Index